This fascinating and inspiring book shows how raw data and personal experience can be distilled into textile art, producing mesmerizing works with deep meaning, whether obvious or hidden, and concentrating on the smaller, quieter moments that make up our lives.

Renowned textile artist and embroidery designer Jordan Cunliffe explores the use of stitched data to tell stories, convey secret messages, and record personal detail, for example daily walks or nightly sleep patterns. Her finished work is beautifully precise, including a long strip of fabric containing a stitch for every day of her life, a reimagination of a favourite childhood book in unreadable code, and pleasing beaded representations of secretly important documents.

Almost any aspect of your life can be represented in graph or map form, and this inspiring book gives you many practical ways to achieve this, whether it's recording the colours of flowers on a favourite path to create your own unique palette, or encoding your most private thoughts in beaded Morse code. It will help you explore new ways of working and develop a fresh new angle in your embroidery and textile work.

Illustrated with a wealth of examples of the author's own work as well as pieces from other data-focused artists from around the world, *Record, Map and Capture in Textile Art* proves beyond all doubt that data can be beautiful, and can inspire stunning works of stitched art.

Record, Map & Capture

in Textile Art

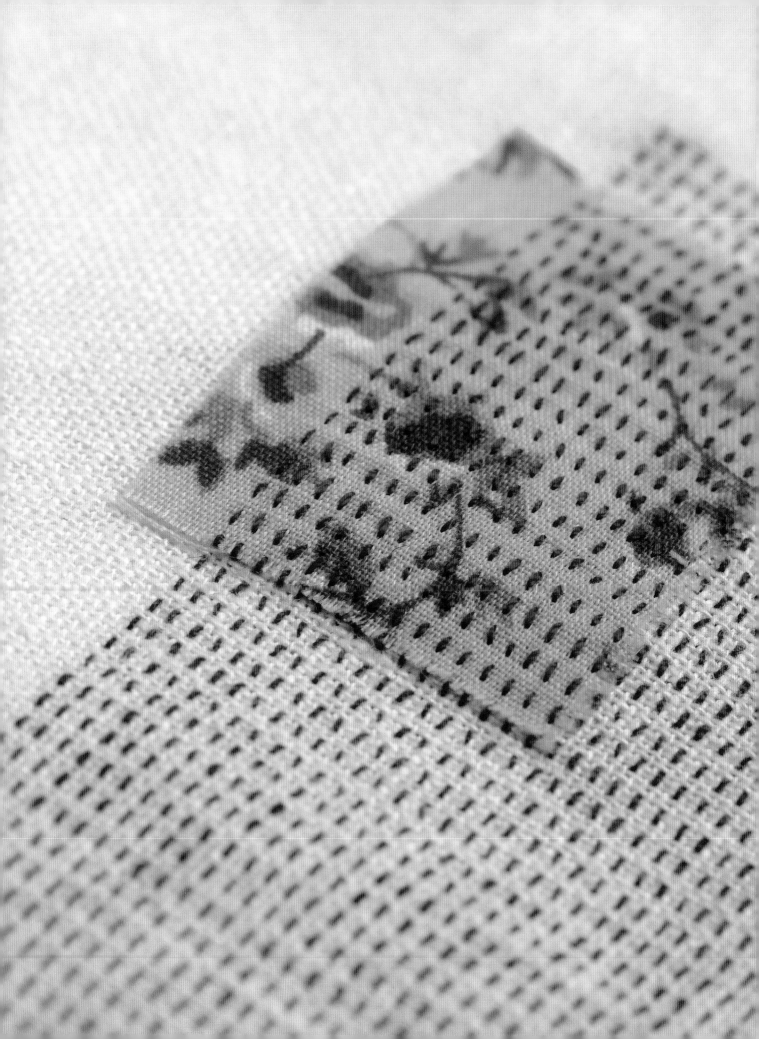

Record, Map & Capture
in Textile Art

Data Visualization in Cloth and Stitch
Jordan Cunliffe

BATSFORD

First published in the United Kingdom
in 2022 by
B. T. Batsford Ltd
43 Great Ormond Street
London
WC1N 3HZ

An imprint of B. T. Batsford Holdings Limited

ISBN 978 1 84994 719 0

A CIP catalogue record for this book is available from the
British Library.

10 9 8 7 6 5 4 3 2 1

Reproduction by Rival Colour Ltd, UK
Printed and bound by Toppan Leefung Printing Ltd, China

Contents

Introduction

'Great things are done by a series of
small things brought together.'

VINCENT VAN GOGH

I have lived most of my life in a small Lancashire town, a place where textile history is woven into the surrounding landscape. Everywhere you turn, there are reminders of the textile industry, from the still-standing chimneys of the long-gone cotton mills, to the soot-blackened bricks of the houses, so indicative of a mill town. My childhood home was built by the local mill owner as a wedding gift for his son, and my own first house, located on the Leeds and Liverpool Canal, was constructed in 1838, most likely for a mill worker. It was built in the view of a looming building, then Brierfield Mill, a steam-powered cotton mill that provided employment for much of the local population.

Research into my family tree reveals textile links everywhere. My great-grandad was the mill manager for a woollen mill in Dewsbury, where a blanket that I still own was produced. My great-uncle emigrated to America after the war and his factory produced the wool for ladies' coats, which he would ship back over the Atlantic Ocean to his sister (my nana). My paternal grandad was a sheep farmer, and I spent many childhood hours in that Yorkshire farmhouse, a place where my granny taught me how to knit, a wonky but cherished scarf emerging stitch by painstaking stitch. Textiles, and their history, are imbued into the fibres that make me, and I have carried a passion for them for as long as I can remember.

During my BA degree course at Manchester School of Art, I found my niche in embroidery. Something about the meticulous nature of hand stitch, and the conventions surrounding this technique, appealed to me, inspiring me to take this age-old tradition and make it my own. Further still, after completing my MA, I discovered a fascination for data visualization, that is the graphic representation of information. This contemporary subject is fast-paced and ever-changing, yet when paired with such a traditional skill as hand embroidery, it becomes laborious and slow and meditative. There is an irony that the data might have changed by the time the stitching is complete.

As my own practice has developed, I have found that the most important elements of my work are storytelling and counting. It must have a meaning; this is the storytelling aspect. I find it easiest to shape my work around a narrative, so I look for stories or 'data' that I want to share, searching for the most efficient way to relay that information through embroidery. More often than not, this narrative relates to everyday life – the smaller, quieter moments that in retrospect can become magnified. I want to give a voice to these junctures and to acknowledge their understated power by taking the time to record them. It is important to me that these moments are recorded meticulously and accurately, which is where 'counting' comes into play: I represent

Visualizing Time project
(detail): see page 56.

6

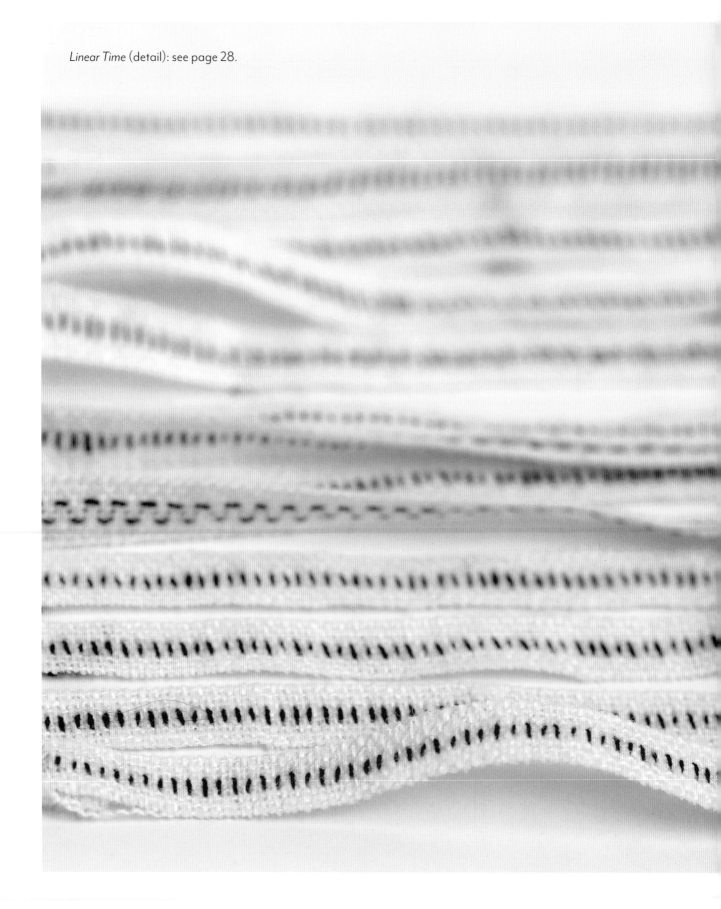

Linear Time (detail): see page 28.

the data in a literal sense, so if I am documenting something that lasted 10,000 days, I will create 10,000 stitches – spending time on something is how I honour it. For this part of the work, the planning is as important as the embroidery, and I consider it to be integral to the artwork.

There are certainly quicker ways to produce the pieces that I make, but I enjoy the work being slow. When every stitch carries meaning, it is important for me to take it stitch by stitch and to consider each one, rather than looking for shortcuts. It also allows me to carve out much-needed thinking time as my hands work to create the repetitive stitches, and I often find that a part of my brain turns to problem-solving when I am in this state, unpicking and untangling the swirling mess of my thoughts until they become as neat and orderly as the stitches on my cloth.

If I am struggling for inspiration, I'll often pick up a needle and thread and start some repetitive stitching. With no destination in mind, I find the activity soothes me and a new idea usually emerges. In the same way that returning to the scene of an event can jog a memory, going back to the familiar action of stitching helps stimulate my thought processes. If you find yourself in a creative slump, or you are struggling to unwind, why not try it too? Set aside a short period of time each day or each week, and keep returning to the same piece of cloth. Let your mind wander, and as you lose yourself in the familiar act of hand stitch, you may well find your creativity.

I focus on the 'everyday' in my embroidery because I want the work to be relatable to everyone. I sometimes keep the descriptions of my pieces deliberately vague, as that way I find that others can find their own story within the stitches. Most of our experiences tend to be universal, after all.

> 'We are more alike, my friends,
> than we are unalike.'
>
> **MAYA ANGELOU**

Materials

'It has been said that next to hunger and thirst, our most basic human need is for storytelling.'

KAHLIL GIBRAN

Although much of my work is data-driven, it is important to me that each piece retains a human aspect. All data is really just storytelling, and because textiles can hold an amazing personal connection, the choice of fabric used can enhance that storytelling capability.

Choice of Fabric

When I create a new piece of work, the first thing I take into consideration is what kind of fabric I will work onto. This always falls into one of two camps: either I choose a sentimental piece of fabric, or I use a grid-based fabric. Here I will discuss the benefits of each through a particular piece of my work, and hopefully these examples will help you as you make decisions of your own.

Sentimental fabric

Whenever I picture my grandad, he is always wearing one of his M&S knitted pullovers, garments he would wear until they fell apart. After he died and we were sorting through his things, I brought one home with me and kept it safe. When I felt ready to honour my grandad's life in stitch, this sweater became the perfect canvas.

It struck me that while Grandad knew me my whole life, I only knew him for a small fraction of his. Sometimes it is easy to forget that people lived entire lives before we knew them, and I wish I had asked my grandad more about his while I had the chance. I decided to commemorate the intertwining of our lives, and in this piece I made a red stitch for every day of his life and a pink stitch for every day of

Grandad's Sweater (2020).
Sentimental knitted sweater, embroidery thread.
610 × 630mm (24 × 24¾in)

mine. It shows all the life he lived before me, where our lives overlapped, and where mine now carries on without him.

As I stitched the red section, I really took the time to consider what my grandad had been doing on each day he had lived. I thought about what his childhood must have been like. I wondered which stitch marked the day that he met my nana, or when his children were born, and which showed the day he moved abroad for work, and did he know at the time how much that would impact the rest of his life?

This is a living monument to my grandad that I can add to, as the time since his passing increases and the pink section grows on its own, weaving my own story into the fabric he wore. Sometimes, when I want to tell a specific story, there is only one piece of textile that will suffice. Perhaps you have similarly sentimental textiles at home that could help you to tell a story?

Below: *Grandad's Sweater* (detail).

Opposite: *The Tiger Who Came to Tea* (2020). Red thread, muslin cloth. 185 × 160 × 30mm (7¼ × 6¼ × 1¼in)

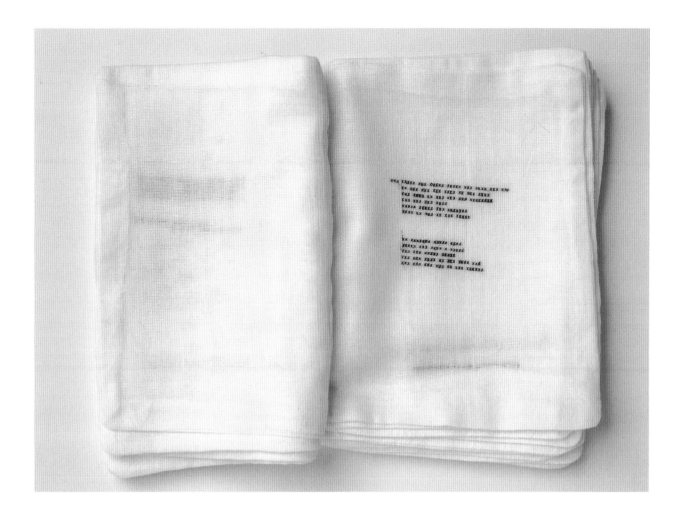

Grid fabric

As a child *The Tiger Who Came to Tea* by Judith Kerr was my favourite book, and when I was around three years old, my parents would find me 'reading' it to myself. Of course, I couldn't read at this point, but I could recite it word for word, and I even knew exactly when to turn the pages.

I wanted to recapture this childhood memory somehow, so I decided to rebuild the book stitch by stitch, sewing a cross for every letter of the story. I wanted this piece to be a direct copy of the book, so each fabric page is the same size as its printed counterpart and the layout, spacing and format of the words are exactly the same as the original text. This was the closest I could get to creating a new 'language' and it was my way of reproducing the experience of 'reading' what was essentially a set of unknown symbols as a three-year-old. I could

simultaneously understand each word, while not actually recognizing it, as the pattern of shapes on the page revealed the story to me. Even now, 30 years later, I can still remember the order and cadence of the words.

Because it was so important to match the original layout of letters, I needed a grid (evenweave) fabric, as this would make it so much easier to measure, count and plot each stitch to ensure the scale and composition correlated precisely to the original book pages. From the evenweave fabrics available, I chose a muslin cloth, because the loose weave of the fabric gave the pages a translucent quality, which meant I could see what was coming on the next page, in the same way that as a child I had known exactly how the story would follow on subsequent pages.

Types of Evenweave Fabric

If there isn't a particular sentimental textile item that I want to stitch onto, then I will always choose an evenweave fabric. To weave a piece of material, warp (vertical) threads and weft (horizontal) threads are crossed over and under each other, and when the thread is evenly spaced on the warp and weft you get an 'evenweave' fabric. I find these grid-like textiles to be really useful for my storytelling pieces, as I can keep an accurate count of the stitches – this precision is integral to the kind of work I do. There are a lot of options, so I like to go to the fabric shop and choose something that has the right scale of grid for my project.

Evenweave fabrics vary in weight, stiffness, texture and colour, so it is good to look around and experiment with a few different types. There are no hard and fast rules about which ones you have to use, but I have listed some of my favourites here. Something to consider is *thread count*, that is the number of threads within a one-inch area of woven fabric. More fine threads can fit into an inch space than coarse threads, which is why, generally, fabric with a high thread count is softer and more supple.

Aida This material is specifically designed for cross-stitch embroidery. It is stiffer than linen fabric, but the holes are easy to stitch through and to keep count of. Aida comes in lots of different colours and a variety of thread counts. The higher the thread count, the smaller the space between the holes. This is an excellent material for a beginner, but as you progress you may want to experiment with other types of evenweave fabric.

Linen This is a natural fabric and therefore has more inconsistencies in the weave (known as slubs) than a manufactured product like aida. Some of the warps and wefts will differ in thickness, meaning your line of stitches may move up and down a bit, but I think this adds a lovely quality to the piece.

Muslin This is a very soft and supple fabric. It has a very open weave, which means that it has a sheer, transparent quality, but it also means it is not very structured, so stitches can pull and may not sit uniformly. Any mistakes on the back of your fabric will show through on the front, so take care to avoid knotted and messy threads.

Aida and linen fabrics.

Other Materials for Embroidery

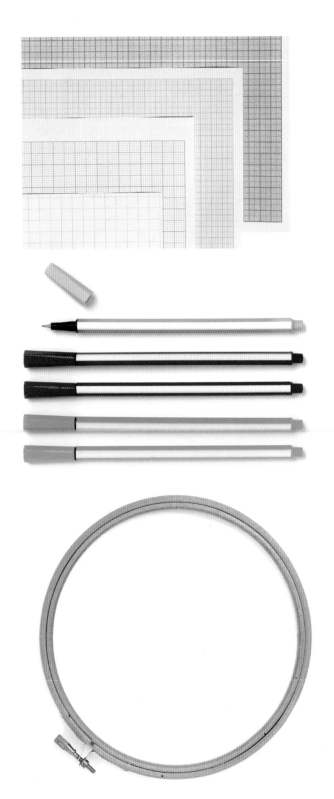

Below are some other materials that I find really useful when I am working on my embroideries, although this list is by no means exhaustive.

Graph paper or grid paper This is really helpful for planning out embroidery designs to give you a pattern to follow when you start stitching. Readily available in pad format in stationery shops, there are also some sheets in the back of this book that you can either photocopy or draw straight onto. The grids come in different sizes so experiment with the scale that works best for your project: if you have a lot of information to plan out, a smaller scale grid that has more squares per page might be best, although you'll find that a larger grid is easier to follow.

Coloured pens or pencils I use different coloured pens to plan my embroideries on graph or grid paper, to help me to keep track of any colour or stitch changes. Fine-liners are especially handy when working on small-scale graph paper.

Erasable fabric pen Sometimes I use one of these to plot out the design directly onto the fabric. Different versions are available: some are removed with water, some with the heat of an iron, and some fade over a period of time.

Embroidery hoop I find it easier to embroider my fabric when it is held in place inside an embroidery hoop, especially if using an evenweave fabric, as it holds the fabric taut, making it easier to follow the grid. This is a matter of personal preference, of course, as not everybody likes to use one, but it will help you to maintain an even tension across your work, which results in neater stitches, so why not give it a try? Hoops come in different materials, sizes and shapes. They can be handheld, clamped to a table or freestanding, and you may find that one is easier to use than another.

Needles Different-sized needles are suited to different kinds of fabric and thread. Basically, you need to make sure your chosen thread can fit through the eye of your needle, but that the needle is no bigger than the holes in your fabric, to prevent fabric distortion. If you are working with beads, you will need to use a special beading needle; this is very fine to allow it to pass through the hole of the bead, but it can be extra tricky to thread!

Scissors Life is so much easier when you have good fabric scissors. I tie a ribbon around the handle of my fabric scissors so they don't get accidentally used for anything else as this can dull the blade. I tend to use larger scissors to cut my fabric, then I keep some small sewing scissors or snips nearby to cut my threads.

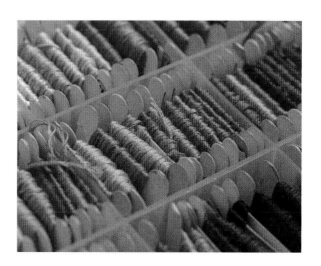

Embroidery thread Also known as stranded cotton or floss, this kind of thread comes in skeins and is made up of six strands that can then be separated depending on how thick you need your stitching thread to be. As my stitches are usually quite small, and I often use a tightly woven fabric, I generally only use one or two strands at a time, which means my thread lasts longer. Stranded cotton comes in lots of different colours, but special effects are available too, such as neon or metallic.

Cotton thread Spooled thread, the kind of thread you would use in your sewing machine, is fine enough to use with a beading needle, and it is also a good option for closely woven fabrics. Available in all the colours of the rainbow, this is an affordable, cost-effective thread that lasts ages.

Data collection tools Although not a necessity, any of the following are useful tools for data collection: smart watches, voice notes on an iPhone, pedometer, camera, journals and diaries.

DIY Project

Life Stories

When you are planning an embroidery project to relate a specific story, remember that the choice of fabric can become part of the story you want to tell. Take the time to consider what textile choices come to mind. If the piece is about someone who is no longer with you, do you have any of their clothes or possessions that you could use? If it is a story from a particular time in your life, do you associate certain fabrics with that period?

Why not have a go at telling a story from your life, paying special attention to the fabrics you use? You could either use an evenweave fabric to count the specific number of stitches needed for your story, or you could choose some sentimental fabric which links to your memories of that time.

You've seen how I used my grandad's sweater as the background canvas to stitch onto in one piece of my work, but what if you only have a scrap of fabric, or if you don't want to use all of it? You can easily incorporate smaller pieces of sentimental textiles into a larger piece of work. This is an example I produced to commemorate the time I spent in a university houseshare, made when I was really missing my friends during the 2020 lockdown; it was the longest time we had ever been apart since our inseparable uni days. Thinking back to when we had all lived together in the house we called Laurel, there were certain fabrics that I strongly associated with that time, including a pair of pyjamas I lived in until I wore them out, and the cheap floral fabric I had used to upcycle some of the old bedroom furniture, to make it feel more like

home. On some basic white linen, I made 3,026 stitches, one for every day since we had moved out of the house. Rather than charting the time we had spent there, I decided to chart the time that had passed since we had left, a lonely time when those happy student days seemed so very far away. I took my sentimental fabrics and incorporated them within the stitches. Living in Laurel with my best friends was such a happy time for me; the days were ordinary, yet extraordinary, and I feel them all come flooding back as I hold onto the fabrics that surrounded me then.

Whenever I come to get rid of textiles, whether it is a fabric that is damaged or clothing I no longer wear, I consider whether I connect any special emotion to it. Often I don't, and I am happy to let it go, but sometimes it stirs up certain feelings and memories. If this is the case, I add it to my fabric stash, and when I am ready to tell that story, I'll bring it back out again.

Not only do these textiles help to illustrate the story I am trying to tell, but certain fabrics hold onto memories that I might have otherwise forgotten. I look back at my trusty old uni pyjamas, for example, and I am transported there: I can smell the house we lived in and I begin to remember things that I had completely forgotten about. Something about that time in my life is imbued within the fibres, and by holding on to the fabric, I am holding on to the memory, until I am ready to commit it to stitch, to be preserved forever.

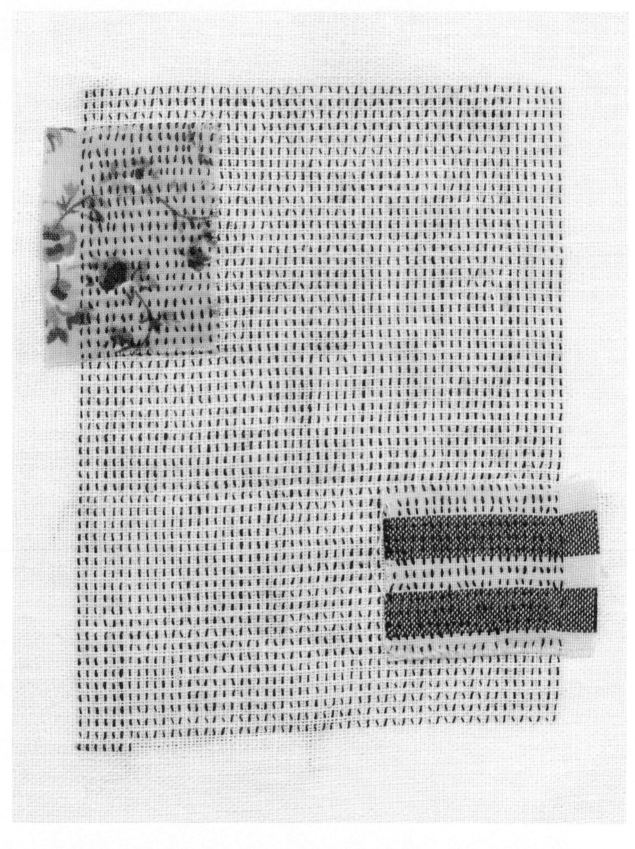

Life Stories project (2021). Linen, red thread, sentimental fabric swatches. 235 x 190mm (9¼ × 7½in)

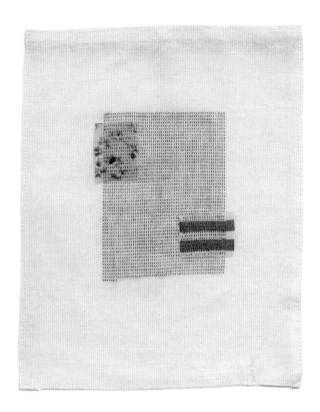
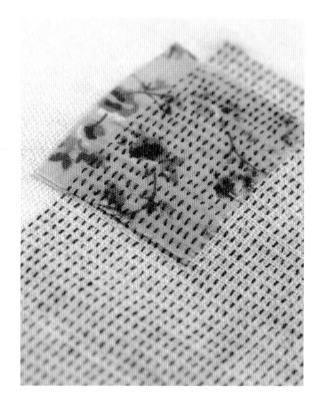

Life Stories project (details).

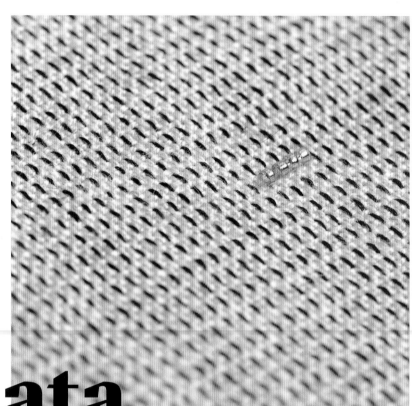

Data
Visualization

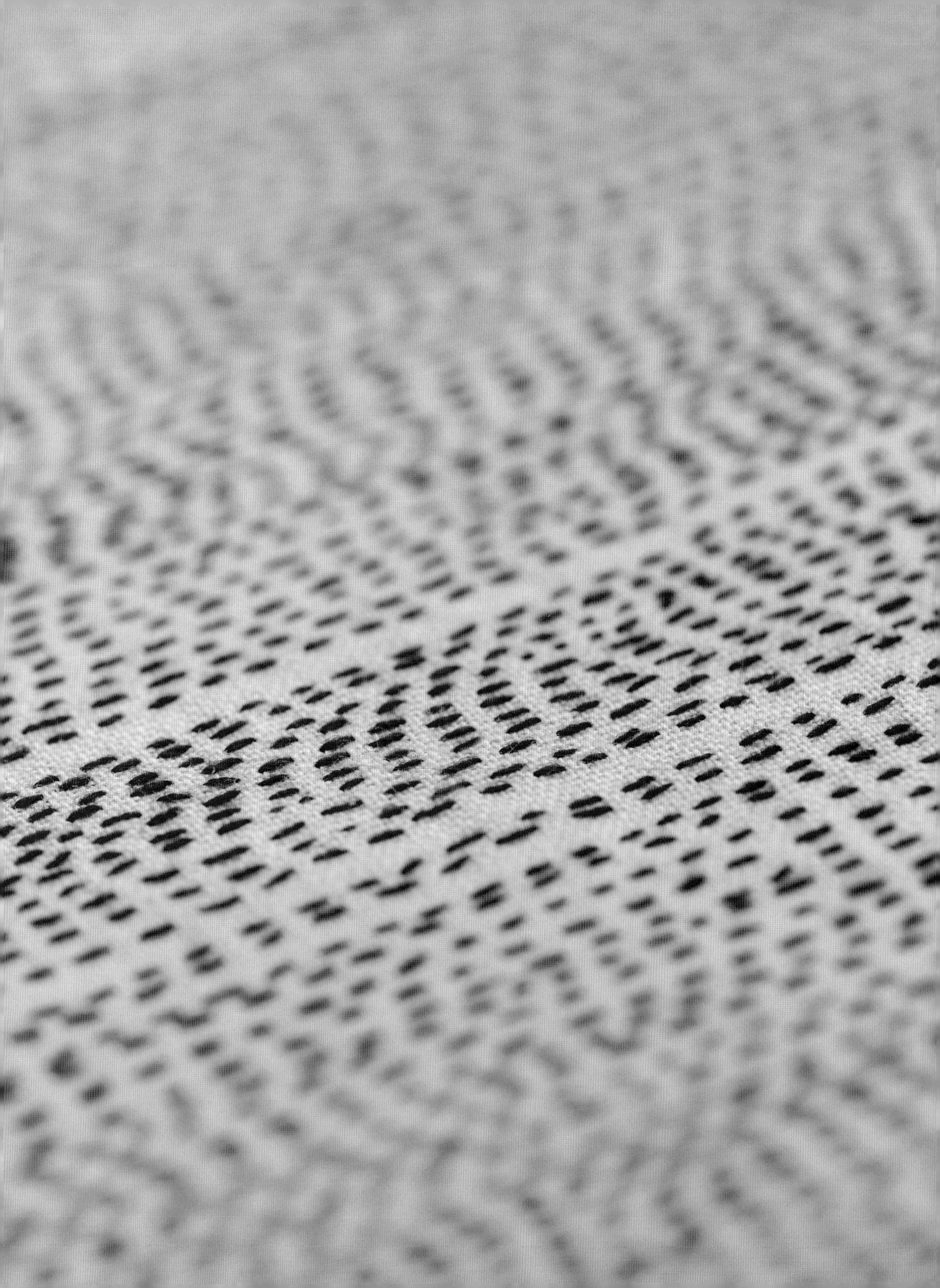

> '**Art is not about art. Art is about life, and that sums it up.**'
>
> **LOUISE BOURGEOIS**

Put simply, data visualization is the graphic representation of information of any kind. Visual data is far easier to digest, and large amounts of material can be shared in a compact way. We are inundated with data visualization every day, in news reports and in advertising, but my research has led me to seek examples in art, specifically through textiles.

The representation of data in a visual form is nothing new: the prehistoric rock art drawings in the Chauvet Cave in the Ardèche region of southern France recorded stories about animals that were encountered over 30,000 years ago, sharing information to aid survival. These images were the natural way for our prehistoric ancestors to communicate with one another.

Fast forward to the present day, and data visualization is still prevalent, an efficient way to process vast swathes of information in this fast-paced world. It is, it seems, human nature to resort to the visual image.

Recording a life

I found myself using data visualization in my work almost by accident. I have an innate need to record and document; it is my way of making sense of the world around me. I like to use a more analogue approach to data visualization: a personal way to chart my personal data. I have always thrived in neatness, and to be able to apply this approach to things I cannot physically touch, such as my thoughts and memories, is incredibly appealing.

I am interested in preserving the 'everyday' and I strongly believe that it is these small, almost insignificant moments that build up to create a rich and meaningful life. There are certain days I could never forget, my wedding day for example, but there are other days that are just as important: a Tuesday when I was 17 years old, walking down by the canal in the sunshine, new shoes giving me blisters on my heels, and the bright blue plasters from the first-aid box at the pub; and later, eating jacket potatoes for tea on our knees, cooked by the woman who would become my mother-in-law. Nothing really happened, but it was one of those important building blocks that has contributed to the life I live now. What if, over time, this memory becomes pushed from my mind because of all the general 'life' admin I need to remember? Maybe there have been other days like this that I have already forgotten without ever knowing it.

If I could save anything from a fire at my house, I would take my embroideries and sketchbooks. There is something about the act of stitching a memory that allows me to unravel my thoughts surrounding an event, giving me a deeper understanding of it that is somehow imbued into the fabric. It would be very difficult to replicate this, even if I re-made the

Sleeping and Waking (detail): see page 34.

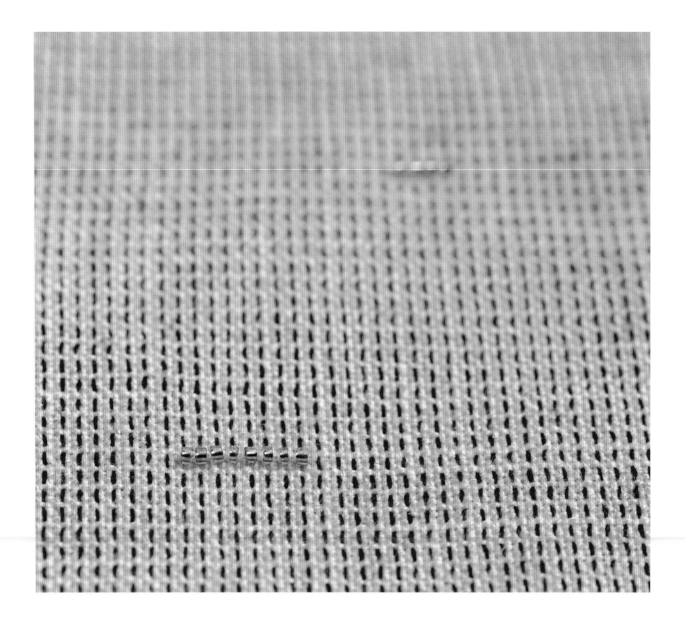

embroidery stitch by stitch. My embroideries become time capsules of how I was feeling in that moment, taking the intangible and making it tangible.

Another component of my recording habit is counting. I have always counted everything, finding it very soothing. When I was homesick during my first year at university, I always knew how many days, hours, minutes until I would be back at home, and I still do it now whenever I find myself in a situation where I don't feel comfortable. Similarly, when I was a runner in my teens, I often used to run a particular route, and I knew exactly how many

steps it would take me to reach the highest point, after which it would all be downhill.

I have a compulsion, it seems, to take the minute details of my life and neatly record them in stitch. I am building up an archive of my life in a code that only I truly understand. Every thought, memory and experience is breathed into these pieces of cloth, giving them a permanence – a place for my consciousness to live on.

Visualizing Time project
(detail): see page 56.

The Bayeux Tapestry

If we take the oversimplified definition of data visualization to mean the visual representation of information, then a lot of textiles throughout history could fall into this category. One notable example would be the Bayeux Tapestry, which, despite its name, is actually an example of embroidery, created in the 11th century to tell the story of the Norman Conquest of England, culminating in the Battle of Hastings in 1066. It measures approximately 70m (230ft) long and 50cm (20in) high, showing the events of the period entirely in picture form. Some historians think it likely that this was because it was intended to be displayed in a church and traditionally imagery rather than text was used for this purpose. As most of the intended audience would have been unable to read, this was the most efficient and direct method of sharing the information.

Now exhibited in a dedicated museum in the town of Bayeux in Normandy, the Bayeux Tapestry is well protected today, but this wasn't always the case. It has been stored and lost and changed hands many times over the centuries, and now over 900 years old, the fact that it is fabric may have contributed to its longevity, enabling it to survive in ways that paper may not have done.

We take this textile piece as an accurate historical document in the same way as we would a written document, and it is considered a primary resource as it was created so close to the time of the events depicted. There is information we can glean from this visual source that may not have been apparent in a written account, such as the architectural styles or types of armour of the day. This textile piece has continued to share its vital information across centuries, ensuring that it isn't lost to time.

Detail from the Bayeux Tapestry.

Linear Time

Time is a universal concept and something that I keep returning to in my work. However much or little of it we may have, it is human nature to measure our lives in time, as much as we may wish that they were measured in terms of our experiences or some other more tangible thing. We all seem to have that ever-ticking clock that makes us wonder what we can fit into the time we have left.

Sometimes, time seems flexible, something that can speed up or slow down, fluctuating between irrelevancy and urgency. As a child, time seemed to spread out ahead of me with no horizon; with no responsibilities and no deadlines, I had no need to keep track of it. In fact, much of my childhood was spent wishing it away, counting down to the next holiday, birthday, Christmas. We are racing towards being a grown-up, daydreaming about the time when we can do as we please, but as we get older, we realize time is in shorter supply. We face new pressures, the need to reach certain milestones at the same time as our peers, wondering if it is too late to start again, with a new dream, a different plan.

When I look back, I see my life in snapshots, the moments that stand out, the key points, and always the most important are the small things, all the mundane moments that build up to make each life unique. I keep coming back to this in my practice, as I try to find ways to adequately express their importance. Sometimes it is difficult to grasp quite how much life we have lived, to keep every moment in our mind, to look at these small snippets and wonder how on earth it can accumulate to (in my case) over 30 years!

Describing time

I began to research the language we use to describe time and I came across the term 'linguistic relativity', the idea that the language used by a particular culture to express the concept of time can affect the way they experience time. The English language, for example, uses expressions such as 'the past is behind us' and 'the future is ahead of us', as we march on at a steady pace. We read time in the same way as we read the words on a page, starting from the left (the past) and working our way across to the right (the future). However, language is a simplification that doesn't take into account the changing pace, the speeding up and slowing down, those times when it feels as if life is swirling around us, or running away from us in all directions.

While in English, time is measured as a distance, with things taking a long or a short time, in other languages, such as Spanish, Greek or Italian, time is less linear and it is discussed using volume-based words, such as large or big, giving it more of a solidity, experiencing it on a more three-dimensional plane.

Does the language we use to describe time explain how we feel about it? Sometimes, we say that time is moving towards us while we stay static: 'Friday is nearly here' or 'Summer is getting closer'. Alternatively, we may describe ourselves as the moving part, where time exists around us and we traverse it: 'We are nearly at the weekend' or 'We will soon be into December'. If you use language that places the self as the moving element, striding through time, do you feel more in control of its

Linear Time (2020). Red cotton on linen. 12,010 × 5mm (472 × ¼in) uncoiled, 90 × 90mm (3½ × 3½in) coiled

effects, as though you can dominate the speed and direction with which you travel? If you use language that describes time 'sneaking up on you' or passing you by, are you more likely to feel overwhelmed by it?

Stitching the work

These were the things I was considering when making this piece. In previous work I had embroidered my time in 'blocks' and I wanted to explore how it might look when it is truly linear. I decided to sew a stitch for each day of my life so far and to display this in one long row. It was difficult to visualize my life in that way and I had no idea when I started how long the piece of embroidery would be.

This piece was fiddly to make. I decided to stitch long rows of individual horizontal stitches onto a piece of fabric, which would then be cut up into strips. This allowed me to work with the fabric in a hoop and it was also helpful in keeping track of the stitches: if I made one length of 200 stitches, for example, I could make the row beside it match and know that I had another 200 stitches, which saved me from having to count every single one!

I started out stitching the number of days of my life up to the point I began the project, but I kept adding a stitch to the running total for every day it took me to complete. This meant that it was a document of my life up until the day I finished stitching, rather than the day I started. The day of completion was 24 July 2020 so, in total, I accumulated 11,197 stitches to represent my life from birth up until that point.

Once all the stitches had been made onto the fabric, I cut the stitched rows into long strips, with each strip measuring 5mm (¼in) wide, using a

sharp Stanley knife and a metal ruler for precision, rather than a pair of scissors. I then hand-stitched the lengths of fabric together, ensuring that the gap between stitches was consistent throughout, even at the end of the rows, as I wanted the stitches to flow in the same rhythm across the whole piece.

Once the piece was fully assembled and I had my 11,197 stitches in a row, I experimented with photography, relating it to my linguistic relativity research. The whole piece stretching out in front of me measured 12,010mm (472¾in) long, so it was impossible for me to photograph at home in one piece. However, it really made me realize the significance of every stitch. Each day I have ever experienced was represented as one red line, the most mundane and the most monumental, side by side, all equally marked in the ups and downs of life.

Next, I looked at how it would fit in a container. I coiled and poked and prodded until the whole length would fit inside a jar roughly the size of a spice jar. It made me wonder what my life would feel like by the time it would fill a jam jar. Does visualizing our life in this way make it more relatable? Certainly, if I put my jar of life side by side with my nana's, it would start to put into perspective the experiences one goes through.

Finally, I coiled the piece up into a flat disc. Perhaps this was just my natural inclination to make it tidy, or perhaps it is a metaphor for my life, the way I try to shrink myself down neatly, to take up as little space as possible. My earliest days carefully nestled away, protected by my more recent experiences. Only once I had done so did I realize that it was reminiscent of a tree trunk. We age trees by cutting them down and counting the rings visible on the stump. Here was my life in neat rings ready to be counted.

Linear Time displayed in a jar.

Sleep

Sleep is often a subject I return to in my work as I find it so intriguing. It is a universal experience that we can all relate to, a constant in our lives. No matter what happens during any 24 hours, we round off each day with sleep, like the punctuation to our daily routine.

When Shakespeare died, he left to his wife in his will his 'second-best bed', a romantic gesture, since their 'best bed' would have been reserved for guests; the second-best bed was where he and his wife slept together. Sleeping time is both personal and vulnerable. We sleep when we are tired, but also when we are unwell, unhappy or overwhelmed.

Our beds are our safe havens and our places of comfort, so the time spent here offers fascinating data to document.

Much of my work revolves around counting, and I have applied the language of counting to sleep tracking for a few different projects in different ways, a couple of which are described below. We are all guilty, no doubt, of counting down the minutes to the alarm when we lie awake at night, and the phrase 'counting sheep' is one we use when we struggle to drift off. Everyone has their own relationship with sleep, but how would your experience of sleep translate into stitch?

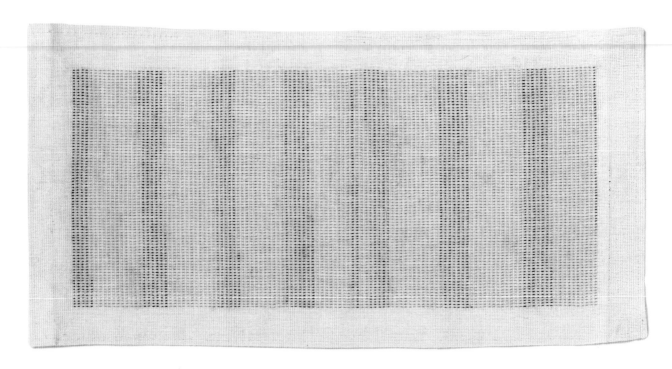

Above/opposite: *Sleeping and Waking* (2017). Black and grey cotton on linen. 310 × 175mm (12¼ × 7in)

32

Sleeping and Waking

I have a Fitbit smart watch that I wear all the time, and one of its features is that it tracks my sleep. I collected this data over a week and translated it into embroidery. Each stitch represents one minute of time: a black stitch for asleep and a grey stitch for awake. Stretching from midnight on Sunday to midnight on Saturday, this piece comprises 10,080 stitches.

Without understanding the code, this piece of embroidery appears soothing, with an undulating rhythm, but once you know what it represents, you begin to notice stretches of waking minutes in the middle of the night, as well as the daytime periods of sheer exhaustion when sleep takes over. Some nighttime awakenings would be forgotten come the morning, were it not for technology keeping a record. Keeping documents such as these helps us to not only capture segments of life, but also to gain an understanding of ourselves.

Sleeping and Waking (detail).

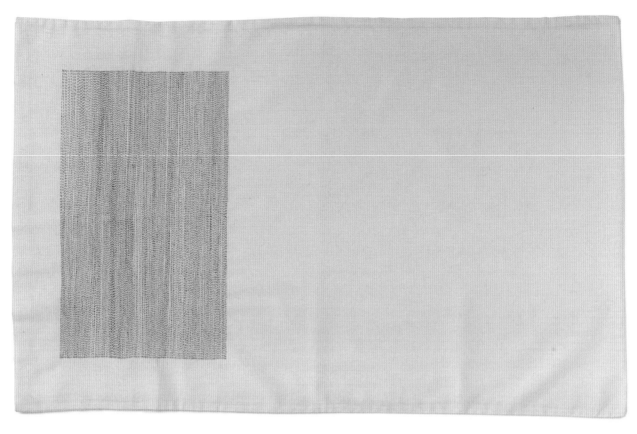

I Could Sleep for a Week

For this piece of embroidery, instead of my usual linen fabrics, I decided to work onto one of our old pillowcases. Whenever I replace my pillowcases, I keep the old ones with my fabric stash, as they encompass 'home' and what it means to me. I have pillowcases from each house I have lived in, bringing them with me when I have moved. All our lives revolve around sleep and these pieces of fabric are my souvenirs.

I Could Sleep for a Week plots a week's worth of sleep. Using my Fitbit again, I calculated the amount of sleep I got in one week at the end of 2020: 55 hours and 13 minutes. Over the space of a few days, I then spent 55 hours and 13 minutes embroidering this pillowcase. This was a different, more literal representation of my data as I 're-lived' a period of my life to create this piece, rather than use each stitch to represent a unit of time. By drawing attention to the time spent on the work, it also serves to highlight the time-consuming nature of embroidery; I could have got a week's worth of sleep in the time it took to sew this piece.

The use of the pillowcase rather than an evenweave fabric means that the stitches are less uniform, the sizes more varied. The piece is inspired by Kantha embroidery, a traditional running stitch technique from India, popular for its handmade aesthetic. The variety in the stitchwork is a more accurate representation of our sleeping lives. This is where we sleep, but also where we have whispered conversations and make our plans. Going to bed is a routine followed each night, it offers a fresh start, and each night is the same but different, just like the stitches. These are the everyday details I want to capture, because these small things are what give our lives depth and meaning.

I Could Sleep for a Week (2020).
Red cotton on pillowcase.
720mm × 450mm (28¼ × 17¾in)

Overlapping Lives

This embroidery charts my relationship with my husband. We were relatively young when we met, and as a result we have grown up together in some ways. I think and measure my life in terms of 'before' and 'after' we got together, because it marks such a fundamental change in the trajectory of my life.

Starting from one end of the fabric, I have made a stitch for every day of my life, and starting from the other end I have made a stitch for every day of my husband's life; in the middle, our lives have overlapped.

It was a time-consuming yet meditative process. When I was sewing my section, I thought about how each stitch represents a full day I have been

in this world: the first few rows of stitches are days of which I have no memory, but what monumental days these were for my mum and dad, as they grappled with the huge life change of becoming new parents; I stitch my way through primary school, and the turbulent teenage days of high school; then, just a couple of months after I celebrate my 17th birthday, as I navigated college, nights out and clutch control, I meet Adam, and everything that I have done since then has been half mine, half his, as we have built a life together. From the other end of my fabric, I do the same for Adam's life, a stitch for every day. But all the days predating our meeting are strange to me, the

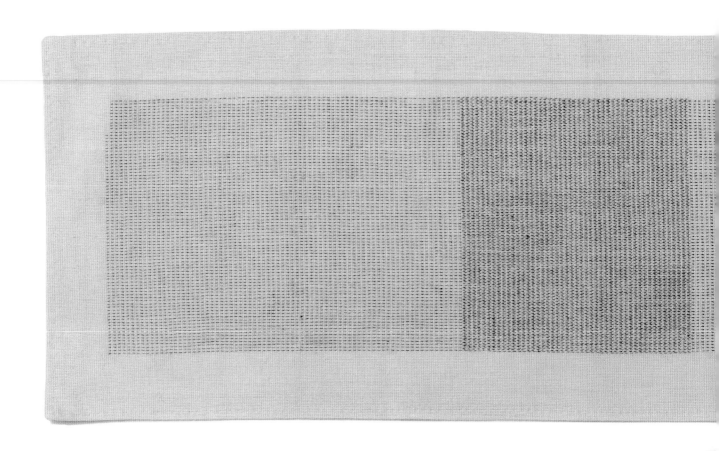

days of a stranger; I have stories and anecdotes and blurry photos that represent this time, but it is charting a life before I entered it. At the centre of the embroidery, our stitches start to merge and overlap, as our lives collided and we became 'us'.

Counting the days

I'm proud of what we have built together, but it is important also to remember that we are individuals with our own stories, as well as the ones we share. This is something I want to get across in the stitch: a sum that is in some ways greater than its parts. I am making a specific number of stitches to represent a specific number of days; I'm not using any kind of creative licence, or trying to give the essence of a particular time, so this becomes something quantitative that I can measure. One of those stitches will show the day I started school, the day I got exam results, the day I lost my first tooth, the days I felt on top of the world, and the days

that were hard. It marks a complete record of every day I have lived since my beginning of time, and as I stitched, I imbued the fabric with those memories and thoughts, committing them to cloth as a permanent record that I was here.

It is difficult to envisage the life of a stranger, which is what Adam was before the day we met. Interestingly, he thinks our paths crossed before that day; he thinks he saw me at parties, and we lived only 10 minutes away from each other; his school teams played against my school teams. We probably went to the same shops, and walked the same streets, and our circle of friends overlaps a little bit at the edges. The chances are we did pass each other, probably more than once. I wonder which stitches show those days?

Every thought, memory and experience I have ever had is wrapped up in this one piece of embroidery.

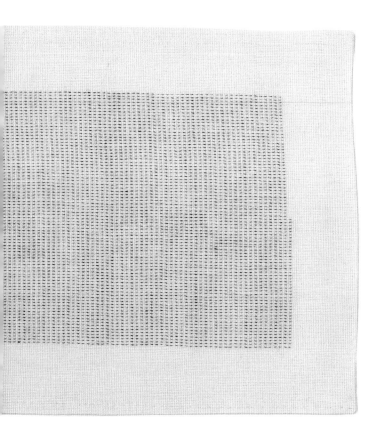

Overlapping Lives (2017). Black and grey cotton on linen. 570 × 190mm (22½ × 7½in)

39

ARTIST'S WORK
—
Laurie Frick

Laurie Frick is a data artist living and working in Austin, Texas, USA. She works with a range of materials to create installation pieces. Her work revolves around the collection of 'everyday' data – the sort of things we can all relate to. This, combined with the familiar materials she uses, helps to make the pieces feel more accessible; we recognize the materials used as the same ones we wear next to our skin or use to furnish our homes, as she explains:

'*Data is like plastic, incredibly useful and horrible at the same time. In the past decade we've gone from being mostly anonymous to almost constantly tracked. Data surrounds us and follows us around. I've looked at all the data collected about us and thought it would eventually be put to good use – to let us see ourselves in ways that are hard to notice or pay attention to. I use familiar materials that are intentionally appealing to pull people into this notion, that data can be human, organic and show us something personal about ourselves.*'

Daily Stress Inventory is based on research that small daily stress adds up to long-term chronic health issues. Laurie collected and charted the small stresses in her life, then allocated each issue a colour and scaled each circle according to the severity of the annoyance. The circles are hand cut from leather and grouped together according to when they occurred, building up a picture of a day. Her hope is that by displaying it in this way, you can take a step back and put some distance between yourself and your stresses. It is interesting to look for patterns within our daily lives, and the best way to do this is if it is laid out visually.

Felt Personality is made up of the data taken from 68,000 user profiles on OK Cupid, collecting responses from relationship and personality questions. Each colour relates to a different

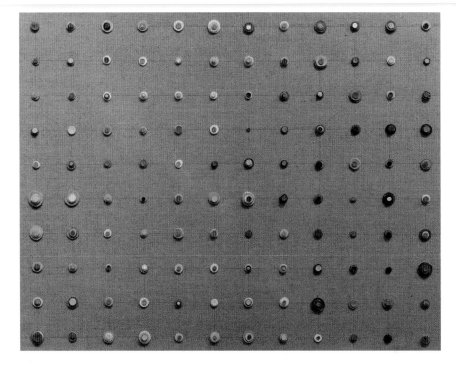
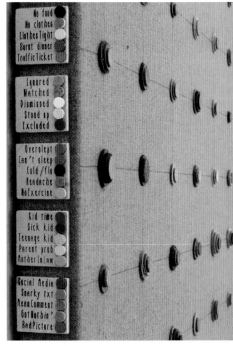

personality quirk and they are categorized based on Murray's system of needs. Murray's system of needs is a system developed by Henry Murray in 1938. This describes how everyone has a set of universal needs, and that the individual importance placed on each need results in differing personalities.

7 Days takes data from the Multinational Time Use Survey, conducted every year, measuring exact daily activities from thousands of individuals. Each activity is given its own leather swatch, and the size of each segment relates to the length of time spent on that activity. The pieces are displayed in days, with the overall installation showing a week's worth of activity in minute detail.

Opposite: Laurie Frick, *Stress Inventory*. Cut leather on stretched linen 71 × 91.5cm (28 × 36in).

Below: Laurie Frick, *7 Days*. Padded leather and aluminium 122 × 122cm (48 × 48in).

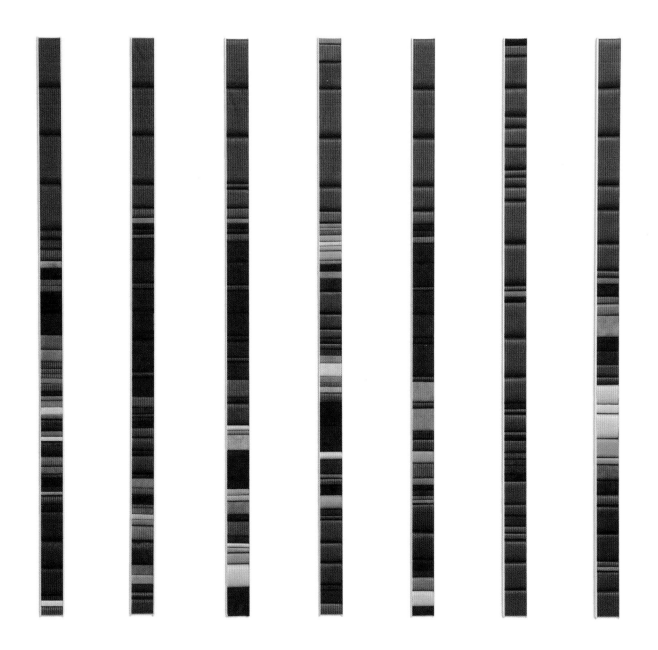

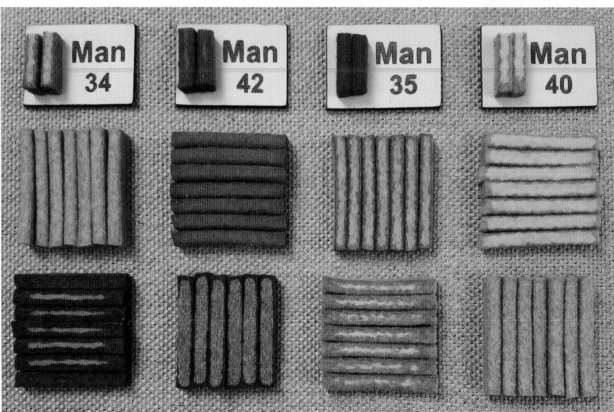

Opposite/above: Laurie Frick, *Felt Personality*. Hand-dyed cut wool felt on stretched linen. 183 × 152.5cm (72 × 60in)

ARTIST'S WORK
—
The Tempestry Project

The Tempestry Project was founded by Asy Connelly, Emily McNeil and Marissa Connelly in the USA in 2017. They were joking about how ephemeral modern data storage is, and the concerns they had that huge amounts of data could disappear at the touch of a button. They suggested that important data sets, such as those about climate change, should be recorded using ancient techniques, such as tapestries, which can last for centuries. Thus, The Tempestry Project was born, 'tempestry' being a portmanteau of 'temperature' and 'tapestry'.

Already anxious and frustrated about the climate change crisis, they set about making a project whereby temperatures (and vitally, how they change over time) could be recorded using knitting. Although temperature blankets already existed, there was no consistent framework in place allowing different pieces of knit to be compared, so they established some parameters.

They developed a spectrum of 32 colours to represent temperatures that ranged from below -31°F (-35°C) to above 121°F (49.4°C), in 5°F (approx. 3°C) increments. This means that any tempestries created can be accurately compared from place to place and time to time.

As we know, climate change is felt more dramatically in places of extreme temperatures, and a trio of tempestries has been created for Utqiagvik, Alaska (the northernmost city in the USA, located north of the Arctic Circle) to represent the years 1925, 2010 and 2016. In 1925 there were 23 days of black knitting – the coldest colour, representing temperatures less than -31°F. In 2010, there was only one, and in 2016 there were none at all. I think that seeing this data visually makes it more relatable. While the tempestries don't always have quite as stark differences as the Utqiagvik examples, climate change can be recognized in how the summers are lengthening and encroaching on the winters, or in how the transition between seasons becomes more abrupt.

An interesting offshoot of The Tempestry Project is the National Parks Tempestry Collection, a range of tempestries knitted by over 100 volunteers, relating to climate data collected from America's national parks. The tempestries are knitted in pairs, comparing two sets of data from two different years, decades apart. Because the coloured yarns are standardized across all tempestries, this allows immediate and direct comparisons of the climate over a period of time, and highlights the effects of climate change in an accessible and understandable way.

A tangible message

Asy has commented that these tempestries make the issue of climate change more accessible to us all. Scientific data often focuses on more remote locations (where temperatures are more extreme), or on future issues such as how the sea levels will be affected in a hundred years' time. Although this data is shocking, it can come across as a bit abstract in relation to our day-to-day lives. These tempestries are created by people to mark the places they live in, at the time in which they are living, making it more tangible, more personal.

The trouble with constant warnings about climate change is that we can become fatigued; we are shocked the first time we hear that it is the hottest April on record, for example, but if we hear this year after year it loses impact. The aim of The Tempestry Project, therefore, is to allow people to connect with climate change on a more personal level. When people see the change in temperature of their own city over their own lifetime, it becomes more 'real'.

The Tempestry Project. This piece shows annual deviation-from-average temperatures, one row per year, from the year 1 AD to 2021. There are roughly 1,950 rows of shades of blue followed by a very sharp red shift.

At one exhibition, a visitor who was a little sceptical about climate change looked at the tempestries from her area, ranging from 1950 to 2016. Temperatures for this area tended to stay in the yellow and orange shades, but she found a week in January 1957 where the temperatures dipped into the blues, and she remembered that week from being a child, when the local lake froze over and she could skate across it. When she examined the rest of the tempestries, she realized that shade of blue never appeared again, a reminder that she had never again been able to skate on that lake. The link between climate change and her own childhood memory was able to educate her about the seriousness of climate change.

Knitting is a laborious activity, and using tempestries rather than the normal display of graphs and written facts to impart climate change information can be beneficial, as even people who don't knit can accept the effort in creating this piece of work. It adds importance to the cause that someone has documented it in this time-consuming way.

Participants in The Tempestry Project have reported that it was a very cathartic and meditative process, allowing them to process their feelings around climate change. Some people chose to knit years that have a significance to them, such as the year of their birth. One woman said that knitting her birth year helped her to feel closer to her mother once she realized that she had given birth during a heatwave, and how difficult that must have been for her.

Creating a tempestry is a form of activism: it brings awareness to this climate crisis we are facing, while making one allows us to spend hours at a time contemplating the issues. The finished tempestries have been taken to marches and demonstrations and carried as banners.

Opposite/below/below right: The Tempestry Project.

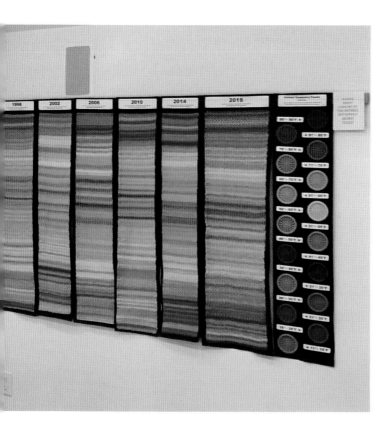

ARTIST'S WORK
—
Olivia Johnson

Olivia Johnson is a designer based in Portland, Oregon, USA. During quarantine she picked up cross stitch as a hobby and has since used it to create the series *Women's Work*, a cross-stitched data visualization project, as a response to the discrimination that women, notably women of colour, continue to face in the workplace.

The medium of cross stitch, a form of art that tends to be labelled as kitsch and as a woman's hobby craft, was intentionally utilized to emphasize the fact that women's labour is routinely dismissed and undervalued. As an art form, cross stitch is often not taken seriously, and Olivia has used this to her advantage, to further emphasize the message that women are undervalued in the workplace.

The *Women's Work* embroideries do not shy away from the fact that they use the traditional cross-stitch technique; they don't try to elevate themselves into a more 'acceptable' art form; they are made using the standard aida fabric, and displayed mounted in embroidery hoops. In the same way that I often use an evenweave fabric for my counted stitch pieces, this aida fabric lends itself to displaying information in graph form; the layout of the stitches makes it easy to compare data across different sets of information.

Although Olivia provides annotated digital versions of her cross-stitch embroideries, which fully explain the data she is exploring, the embroideries themselves have enough of a graph-like form that even at first glance, it is clear that they have information to share. They are not disguised as decorative motifs, nor do they try and alter the recognizable shapes of pie charts and bar charts. This makes it abundantly clear from the outset that they are data visualizations of some kind, and invites the viewer to make a closer inspection.

Data about women being undervalued and underrepresented in the workplace is nothing new, but this novel way of displaying the information, subverting the role of the cross-stitch craft to women's own advantage, is certain to catch the attention in a way that a digital presentation cannot.

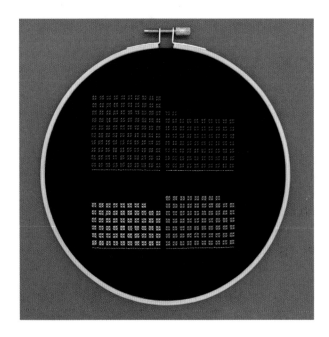

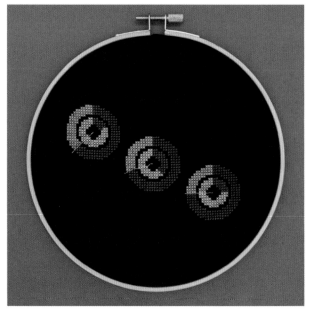

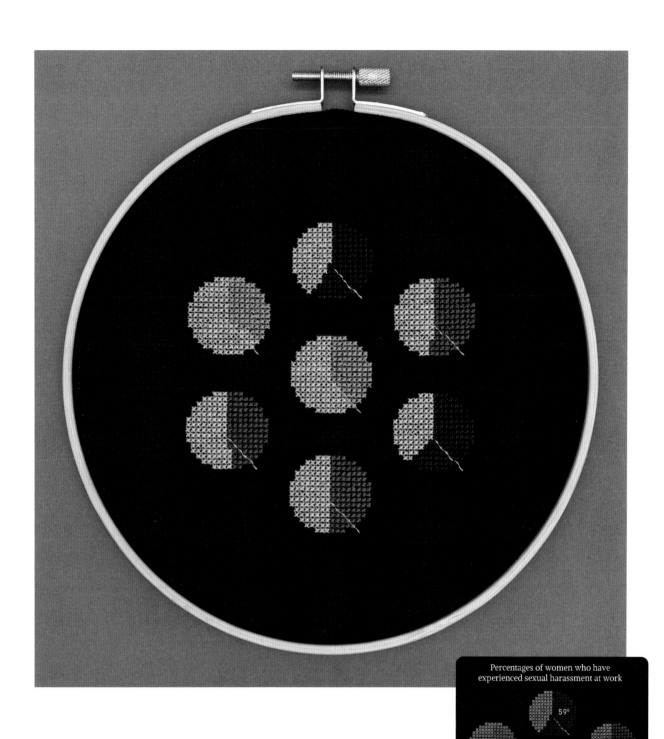

Opposite/above/right: Olivia Johnson, *Women's Work*. Cross-stitch embroidery on black aida cloth, mounted in an embroidery hoop. 18cm (7in) diameter

Percentages of women who have experienced sexual harassment at work

34% WOMEN OF COLOR

59% SENIOR-LEVEL WOMEN

53% LESBIAN WOMEN

48% WOMEN IN TECHNICAL ROLES

41% ALL WOMEN

62% BISEXUAL WOMEN

51% WOMEN WITH DISABILITIES

ARTIST'S WORK
—
Ahree Lee

Ahree Lee is a multi-disciplinary artist based in Los Angeles, California, USA. Two of her pieces in particular stood out for me while I was researching textile data visualizations. They are in and of themselves beautiful stand-alone pieces of woven textiles, but the meaning behind them gives another dimension to the work. I like the fact that Ahree is very precise in her practice, tracking data exactly and recording it meticulously. Her work ranges from pieces that rely on very personal data (*Timesheet: November 4–10, 2018*) to those based on widely relatable data not taken from her own life (*Disrupting the Industry*). Of *Disrupting the Industry*, Ahree says:

'*Disrupting the Industry is a woven graph visualizing the rise and fall of the percentage of computer science bachelor's degrees earned by women from 1966 to 2010. Despite a peak at 1984, marked in the weaving*

by a band of copper wire, by 2010 the level had dropped to almost where it was in 1966.

A number of factors have been posited as contributing to this drop, including the image of the nerdy boy hacker popularized in such films as War Games, and enrollment caps on computer science majors that limited access to those with prior computing experience – most often boys whose fathers had bought them newly available personal computers like the Apple IIe. Industry disruption is a Silicon Valley ideal and promised by tech company founders to potential funders. But what they often fail to consider is the subsequent disruption to society.'

Above: Ahree Lee, *Timesheet: November 4–10, 2018*. Cotton, linen, wool, viscose, rayon and polyester. 101.6 × 178cm (40 × 70in)

Opposite: Ahree Lee, *Disrupting the Industry*. Cotton, linen and copper on canvas. 30.5 × 30.5cm (12 × 12in)

Of *Timesheet: November 4–10, 2018*, Ahree says:

'In the fall of 2018, I kept track of what I was doing all day long in a spreadsheet. Each activity I assigned to one of half a dozen different categories, including childcare, housework, art practice, and sleep. I picked one week of that time period and during the course of my artist residency at the Feminist Center for Creative Work in Los Angeles, turned it into a series of seven weavings, one representing each day of that week. I wove them during weekly studio hours, on my floor loom that I moved into the space for the exhibition. By giving these ephemeral activities form through my weaving, I have created an analogue data visualization of invisible and undervalued domestic labour and transformed it into an artwork with monetary and cultural value.'

DIY Project

A Day in the Life

If you want to make your own piece of stitched data visualization, a good way to begin is to plot a day in your life. This could be a special day that you want to commemorate, or just your ordinary routine; whichever you choose, use a stitch to represent each minute of the day.

Think about the sort of information you'd like to preserve and how you want to represent your day: it could be a record of activities, such as travel, socializing and work; or a barometer of your mood: happy, sad, anxious or excited. You might want to track your sleeping and waking hours, or who you spend time with – it can be anything that is important to you.

If you choose to record your day-to-day activities, say, make a note of how you spend each minute of your chosen day, and assign each activity a different colour of thread. If you have a phone that allows you to take screenshots, it can be helpful to screenshot your home screen to show the clock when you change activities, as this lets you keep track of timings when you are on the move.

Before I begin stitching, I find it easiest to plot my design out on paper first. Use the graph paper in the back of this book and chart the minutes of your day with coloured pens. Work from midnight to midnight. There are 1,440 minutes in a day, which can be set out as a block of stitches 30 wide by 48 high. There are other formations that work, too, but by following this pattern each horizontal row

of stitches represents half an hour, which I find is much easier to keep track of.

I have done this exercise, or variations of it, several times. And although I am fastidious about keeping track of my minutes, it isn't unusual for me to have minutes 'missing' – it could be that I have forgotten to make a note, but often I am just moving between activities, the few minutes, for example, that I spend walking from my bed (sleeping) to the kitchen (eating). You may want to allocate a colour to these 'in-between' times, but I prefer to leave spaces in the fabric, as I like the rhythm it creates on the cloth.

Below are the specific activities I tracked on my day and the colours I have used to represent them:

- **Sleeping:** Black
- **Working:** Navy blue
- **Eating:** Pale blue
- **Watching TV:** Grey
- **Socializing:** Green
- **Exercising:** Red

My finished stitching measures 60 x 100mm (2⅜ x 4in), but this will vary depending on the weave of the fabric you choose to stitch on, or the size of your stitches.

Use these instructions as a rough guide to help you plan many different kinds of data visualizations. Explore the idea of collecting different sets of data,

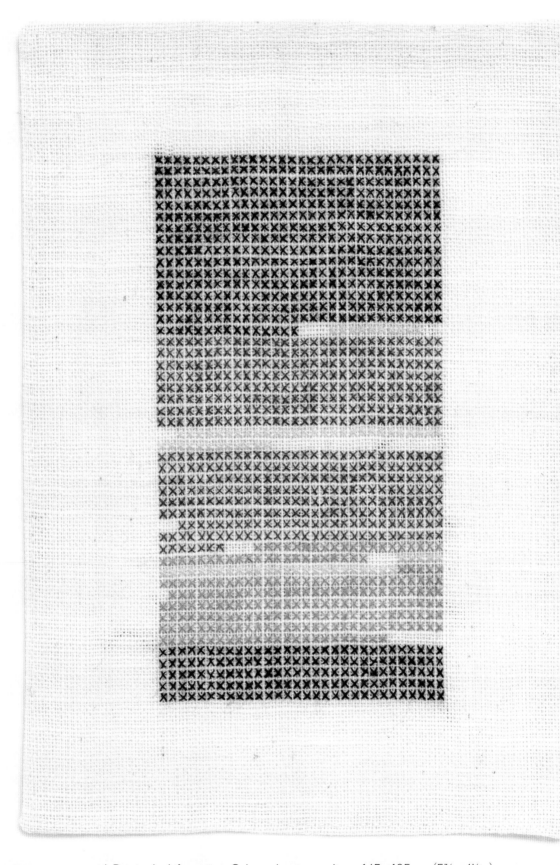

A Day in the Life project. Coloured cotton on linen. 145 × 105mm (5¾ × 4¼in)

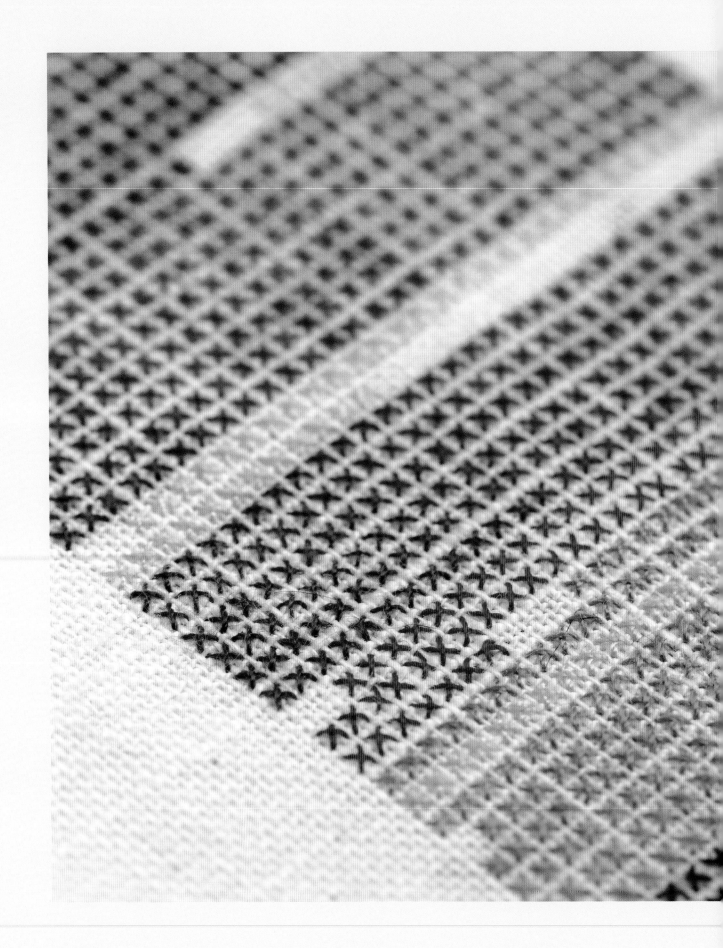

or swap around the format of the stitches to make your block of embroidery square, or longer and thinner, portrait or landscape. Change your colour palette, or maybe use beads and sequins instead of coloured threads. You could even vary your stitch type to represent the different activities, rather than changing the colour of your threads, creating a stitch 'sampler' of your day that has a similarity to a traditional embroidered sampler.

Repeat the exercise across a few days for comparison, or recreate the same piece for the same day each year and see how the rhythms of your life change. Explore the different possibilities of charting your life through stitch.

Left: A Day in the Life project (detail).

Below: The design plotted out on graph paper.

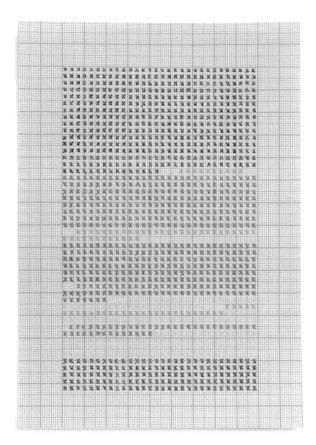

DIY Project

Visualizing Time

Many of my data visualizations relate to the subject of time. I find being able to 'capture' a significant period of time very valuable. If you want to make your own time visualization, first decide what time period you want to commemorate. How has your life been divided up so far and which chunks of time were the most meaningful to you? It might be your university years, or time spent in a certain job, or maybe something shorter, such as a pregnancy, or the length of your wedding ceremony (either could make a lovely sentimental gift for a loved one, too).

Once you have chosen what you would like to visualize, decide on the best unit of time to use. Each stitch could represent one week, one day or one minute. What would be the most appropriate for your project? This will determine the overall size of the piece, as well as how long it might take to stitch.

Consider opportunities to make your piece even more personal, by adding extra detail through use of colour or material. For example, if you were plotting a relationship, you might want to change thread colour to mark the point at which you got married, moved house, or welcomed a child. There might have been especially significant days that warrant extra attention, so maybe you will mark these days with a bead (but try to find beads that

Visualizing Time project (detail).

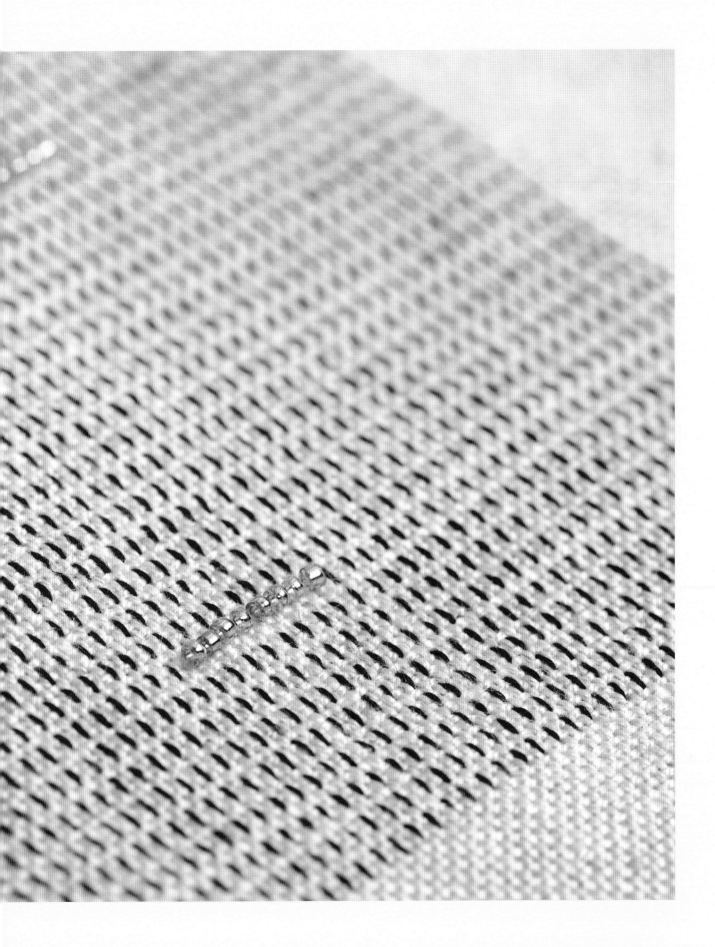

The design planned out on paper before stitching.

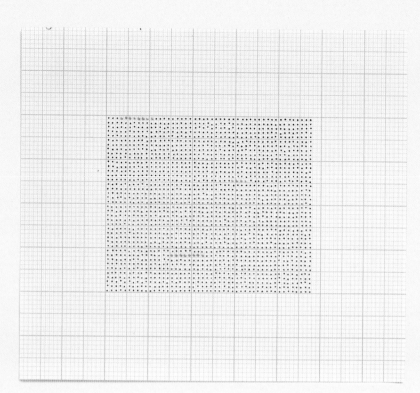

are the same scale as your stitches, otherwise it can throw off your pattern). If you keep a diary, look through past years to make sure you have captured all the most important dates. You understand your time better than anyone, so make sure that your piece preserves what is important to you.

Plotting out

Once you have gathered all of your data, it is time to start plotting out the embroidery. I find it easiest to start with a pen and paper and list the dates I want to include in chronological order, and then I draw it out onto graph paper so it is easier to follow when I start to sew. This way of working also gives you the opportunity to play around with format, to see if you would prefer the stitching to be landscape, portrait or square. You can also see if you can fit your stitches into a solid block, although this may not always be possible depending on the number of stitches you have to work with. If you are making thread colour changes or special stitches, mark these with different coloured pens on your graph paper plan, so that it is really clear when you start sewing. In this planning stage, there are websites such as www.timeanddate.com where you

can input two dates and it will calculate the duration between them in different units of time, such as weeks, days, hours, etc., which can be really useful.

Starting to stitch

When the embroidery has been all planned out, you are ready to start stitching. An evenweave fabric often works best as you can keep track of each stitch as well as keeping them aligned, but if you have some fabric that is reminiscent of the time you want to represent, an item of clothing or a home textile perhaps, now could be a good time to use it, to make the storytelling even stronger.

In my example, I have chosen to represent my marriage. I decided to use one stitch to represent each day, working out at 1,920 stitches, which would divide evenly into a block of stitches 48 wide by 40 high. I have used a basic straight stitch, starting with blue thread, then swapping to red to mark the date we moved into our house. We have taken three really special trips during our marriage, starting with our honeymoon, and I have marked these using beads.

So, decide what you want to represent and what will make it really personal, then enjoy bringing your story to life using the stitches you like to work with.

Visualizing Time project. Blue and red cotton and gold beads on linen. 165 × 140mm (6½ × 5½in)

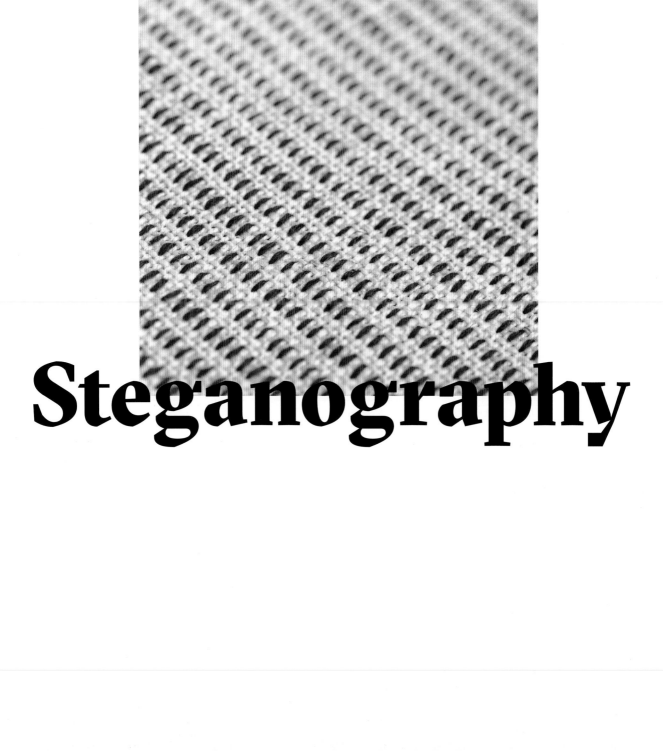

Steganography

> '*Artists are people driven by the tension between the desire to communicate and the desire to hide.*'
>
> **D. W. WINNICOTT**

The word 'steganography' refers to the act of concealing secret information within something public, in order to avoid detection. In other words, hiding something in plain sight. This often refers to data that is hidden within computer programming, but I have found several examples of it within the textile world, too – in fact, I was working in this way before I even knew the word.

My work is a constant balancing act between wanting to share very personal information and desperately needing privacy, and the way I get around this is to conceal or disguise the data I am sharing. A lot of my work has manifested itself in this way: the pieces appear to be simple rows of stitch, but they always have a meaning, and it is then my decision whether to share this meaning (or code) with others.

Steganography goes a step further, by actually encoding the information rather than just 'representing' information in stitch. This means that a code is followed to create the work, and so this has the potential to be decoded in the future to reveal the message. In this way, you can have something very personal on full display, but nobody else would understand it unless you made the decision to share. I think that having something secret like this can foster a closeness between the parties who understand.

As my work has evolved from purely sharing my own stories to sharing the stories of others, I need to be mindful that not everyone is comfortable with having their personal anecdotes out in the world. Steganography allows information to be both concealed and revealed.

Scrabble Alphabet (detail):
see page 71.

Steganography in Wartime

The embroidered samplers of Major Alexis Casdagli

Major Alexis Casdagli was a British officer taken prisoner by the Nazis in 1941 during the Second World War. To pass the long hours in the prison camp, he was permitted to sew various embroidered samplers. Without access to threads, the samplers were made from yarns pulled from various items of clothing. The samplers he created were well liked by his captors, so much so that they were displayed on the walls of the prison camp for four years, and his skill in embroidery was such that he was permitted to teach the other inmates to stitch.

It was only after the war that one of these embroidered samplers was examined more closely, revealing its secret message. Appearing at first to be a traditional sampler embroidered with his name, the date and a decorative border of cross stitches, the unevenly spaced border stitches were, in fact, messages written in Morse code, one reading 'God Save the King' and the other, slightly riskier, 'Fuck Hitler'. A notable example of textile steganography.

Major Casdagli credited this gentle resistance with keeping him sane during his lengthy time in captivity. At the back of this book, you will find a Morse code alphabet if you, too, want to create your own secret message in this way.

Knitted espionage

Knitting is a perfect vehicle for steganography because, in essence, it consists entirely of two types of stitches (knit and purl), which lend themselves perfectly to binary code. It can also be applied to Morse code by adding knots to the yarn, which proved especially useful during the Second World War. Knitting was encouraged at the time, so that women could contribute to the war effort. Wartime propaganda campaigns encouraged knitting groups to knit for the soldiers, so seeing a woman knitting was not an uncommon sight, nor did it arouse suspicion. There was a prevalent, sexist view that women were not to be taken as seriously as men, and in fact state secrets were openly shared in front of them, something that the British War Office used to their advantage. Due to the nature of this topic, and its links to wartime spies, it is difficult to get accurate anecdotal testimonies about exactly what happened, but the following seem to be widely accepted as fact.

During the Second World War, the British Government employed Phyllis Latour Doyle to gather intelligence on the German troops. Doyle would cycle around the Normandy countryside posing as a tourist, chatting with the Germans and collecting information. In order to report back her findings, she carried with her a length of silk yarn which was knotted with her 'codes', and to make it look less conspicuous, she kept this yarn together with a pair of knitting needles, disguising it as an innocent hobby. She is said to have used this method to pass more than 100 coded messages to British intelligence officers and she was never detected.

Back in the First World War, the Belgian Resistance had employed similar tactics against the occupying Germans. They would recruit women whose homes overlooked train yards, and they would be asked to sit by the window and knit. Instead of just making clothes, however, their knitting would contain hidden messages, such as a dropped stitch to indicate one type of train passing, or a purl stitch to indicate another, keeping the Resistance informed of the schedules of enemy transport and allowing them to track their logistics.

Major Casdagli's sampler.

Examples of knitting espionage date back even further than this, to the American Revolutionary War of 1775–83. Molly Rinker owned a tavern where British soldiers would come to drink, and as she overheard their conversations, she would write them down, hiding the messages in balls of yarn, which she dropped off a cliff to be collected by the American soldiers waiting below.

All of these women, Molly Rinker, Phyllis Latour Doyle, the Belgian knitting grandmothers and no doubt many others, were able to go undetected by virtue of being women, paid so little heed that their enemies would openly discuss confidential information right in front of them, meaning that these female spies could relay this information back to their troops.

During the Second World War, however, the Office of Censorship in the USA and in Britain did ban the sending of knitting patterns in international post, for fear that people may be sharing secret codes. If you don't knit, you will probably appreciate how the patterns with their abbreviations and shorthand instructions could look like some kind of hidden cypher. In fact, this idea was also explored in Charles Dickens' 1859 novel, *A Tale of Two Cities*. Set in revolutionary France, his bloodthirsty character Madame Defarge would keep a 'knitted register', where she recorded the names and descriptions of the French nobles next to face the guillotine, often under the eyes of her victims.

21.3.2001: A Binary Beaded Diary

I created a piece of binary code embroidery in order to share the contents of my childhood diaries. I kept a diary meticulously when I was younger, as a way to keep track of my seemingly dramatic life – mortifyingly hilarious to look back on now. In the interest of preserving the privacy and modesty of my much younger self, I wanted to find a way to encode the information before I shared it with the wider world. Of course, someone who understands binary code would be able to translate it back into plain English – but it's not like I am trying to hide anything truly secret, just the trials and tribulations of an 11-year-old girl.

I used a free binary code translator service I found online to type in my diary entries, and it was translated into a series of '0's and '1's. I assigned black and grey beads respectively to the code and began the painstaking task of stitching out the entry. In binary code, each letter of the alphabet is represented using a sequence of eight '0's and '1's, so a four-letter word is suddenly made up of 32 characters, making my diary entries significantly longer than they were to begin with, hence the very time-consuming task.

My diaries were small, pocket-sized ones that only allowed for a few lines of writing per day, so the younger me really had to edit down what I was going to feature in each entry. The pockets of information I chose to share seem so insignificant to me now that I am an adult. Things like which seat I chose on the school bus, or who I texted. The hierarchy of important events seems skewed when I look back over those pages. To make the best use of the limited space, there are a plethora of abbreviations and symbols I barely recognize now,

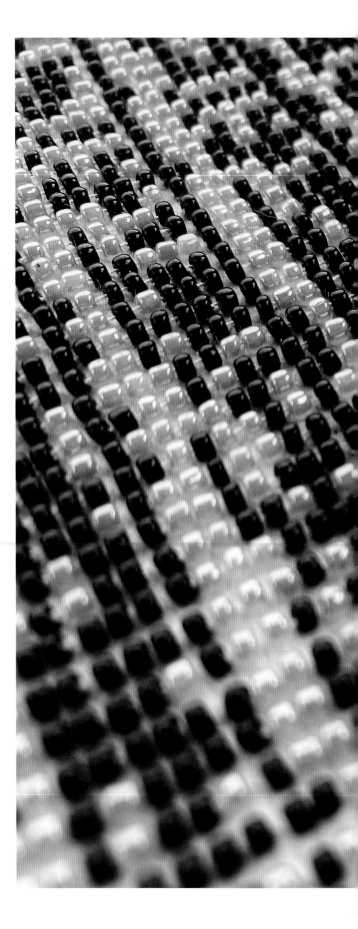

Binary Beaded Diary (detail).

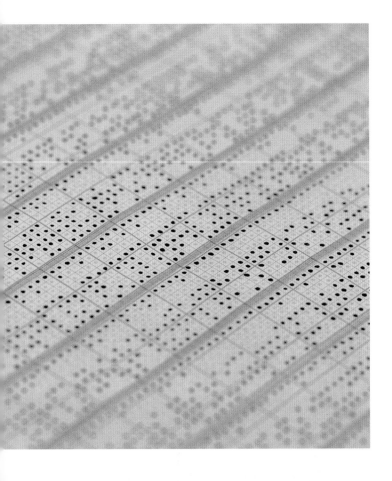

but that were probably second nature at the time, due to the limited number of characters available on a pay-as-you-go text message. I have included both the abbreviations and the spelling mistakes of my younger self, to create a true reflection.

The entries veer between the theatrical and the mundane, laying bare the inner workings of my childhood mind. Some of the names that feature frequently have completely dropped off my radar. These childhood friends remain frozen in time, trapped between the pages. The memorable encounters deemed worthy of mention make this little time capsule all the more poignant, and leave me wondering how many childhood memories of others I may feature in, events or occasions, perhaps, that I don't remember at all.

Waves of nostalgia wash over me as I take in the sight of my childhood handwriting, so familiar and yet so alien. My carefully constructed ampersands meticulously copied from an older girl, lapsing into normal plus signs when I was in a rush. As soon as I open the pages, I suddenly remember the smell of my blueberry gel pen, although the scent has long since faded. I later invested in larger journals with more space to write, but there's something so lovely about these little diary entries, with their sense of the unwritten being as important as what did make it into ink.

Now my diaries are purely functional, birthdays, anniversaries, appointments and to-do lists. Devoid of emotion, my stitch becomes my daily narrative. But I wonder, in 20 years' time will I miss having something written to look back on?

As I had not worked extensively with beading in the past, I was pleasantly surprised by the weight of the finished piece, my usual embroidery stitches being virtually weightless. It gives it a special quality as it flows between my hands, carrying the weight of all those hidden words that I thought important enough to immortalize in those little diaries.

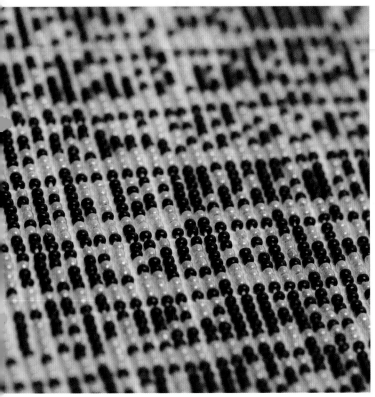

Above left: the diary plotted out in binary code. Opposite: *Binary Beaded Diary* (2017). Black and grey beads on even-weave fabric. 140 × 190mm (5½ × 7½in). Detail shown left.

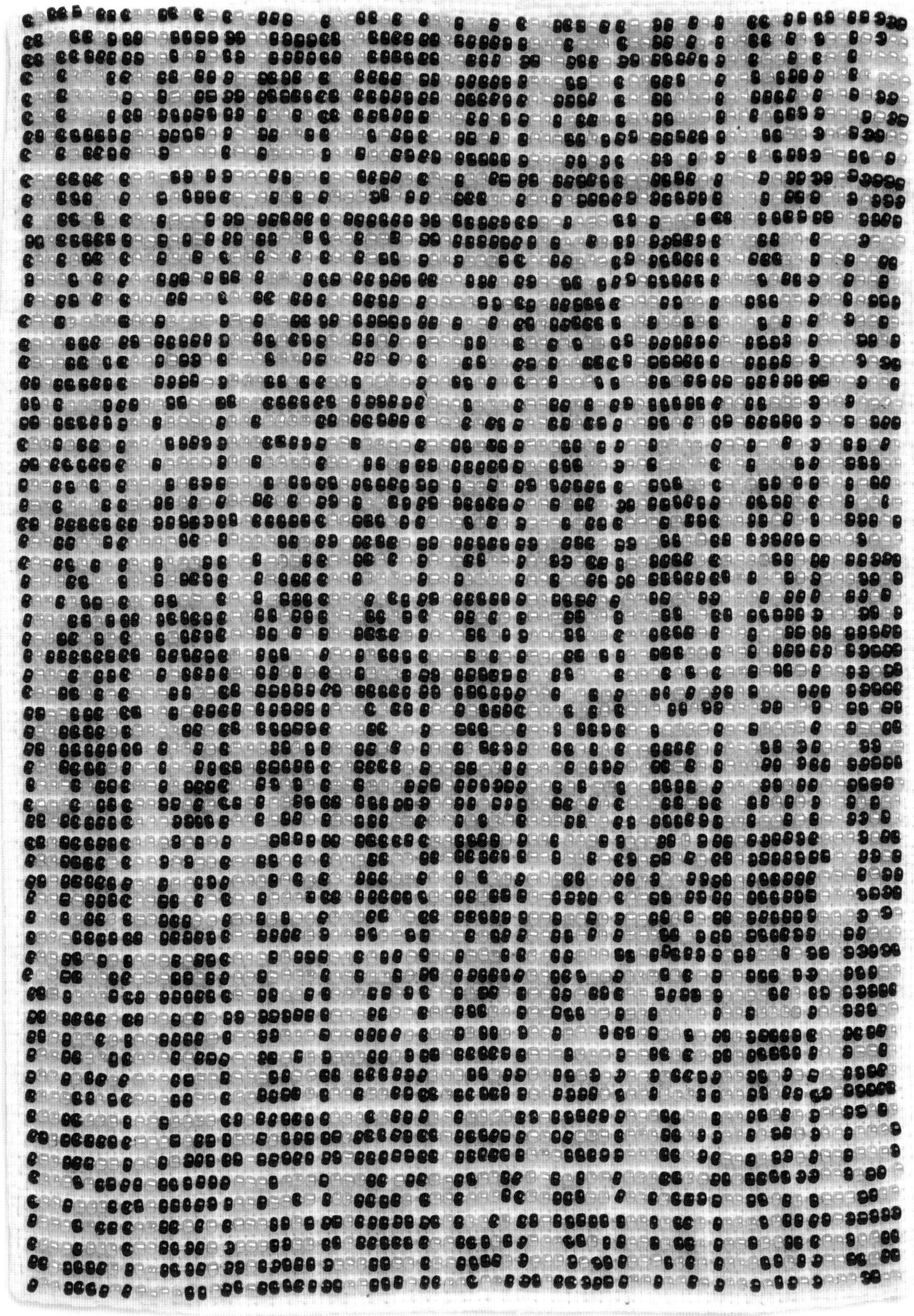

A

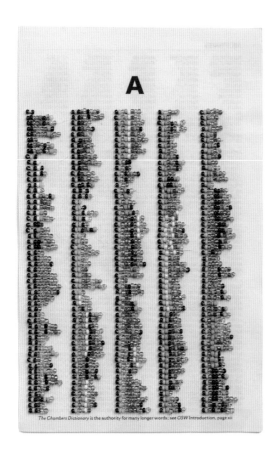

B

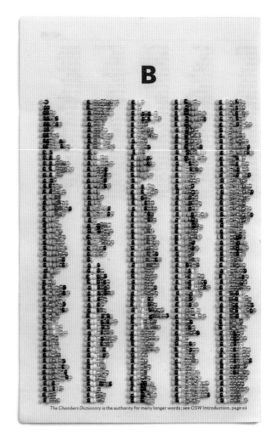

C

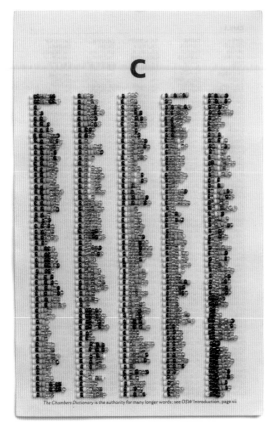

D

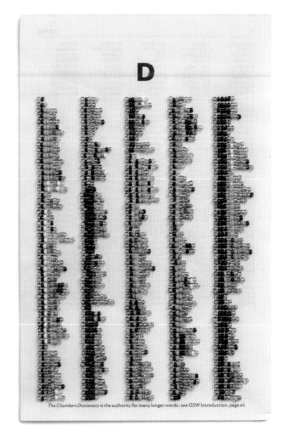

Coded Alphabet

I found a book in a charity shop called *Chambers Official Scrabble Words 4th Edition*, which lists alphabetically every accepted word for a game of Scrabble. Although written in English, it was a bit like reading a foreign language; there were so many words I didn't recognize that I ended up letting them wash over me without comprehension, but something about the way the words were laid out on the page, their varying lengths and the alphabetical order, drew me in. So I decided to create some work based on this new language.

Firstly, using my bead collection, I allocated a different coloured bead to every letter of the alphabet. I chose beads that were a similar scale to the printed letters in the book, selecting colours that were sufficiently different so that the letters wouldn't get mixed up. Then I began the painstaking task of stitching a bead over every letter in each word.

What emerged were beautiful collections of shiny coloured beads arranged in a seemingly random order, or so it would seem to a viewer with no understanding of the project, but I was actually creating my own visual colourful language. I began to 'read' in beads and I could recognize words from their beaded configuration. If you studied them for long enough, you could probably crack the code, as the words are in alphabetical order and you would start to find patterns emerging within the shapes.

In fact, there was something quite freeing about working in this way. In the next chapter, Algorithms, I discuss how working to a set protocol can release us from decision-making, and that was what was happening here. I don't use a lot of colour in my work – many of my pieces are monochromatic – but

this series is riotously colourful. If I was choosing the placement of each coloured bead, I would overthink every decision, but the fact that the colours were predetermined took that pressure off. I didn't need to worry if one colour didn't really look great next to another as it wasn't my fault; each bead had a purpose and needed to be in the place that it was.

If I had thought about it more up front, or if had I known that I would continue this project past the letter 'A', I might have started to consider which letters would appear more frequently and which were more likely to appear side by side, but in actual fact the decision-making was incredibly arbitrary, determined by nothing more than the order in which I had pulled the beads out of the drawer. Now the language has been formed, and there is no opportunity to alter or amend.

Taking it further

I enjoyed creating this project, but I wanted to take it further than the Scrabble alphabet. I have found that my most successful embroideries are pieces that are personal to me, so I decided to apply this new language to encode some personal correspondence. Although this information isn't something I would necessarily want to share, I feel confident that by using my new code the details will stay private. While I have hidden its content, I like the fact that it probably can be recognized as a letter. There are certain constructs, such as the address at the top right, then the left alignment of the body of text below, the spaces top and bottom that allude to a greeting and sign off, even the folds in the paper that let us know what kind of envelope it arrived in,

Scrabble Alphabet (2020). Multi-coloured beads on found paper. 194 × 120mm (7¾ × 4¾in) (×4)

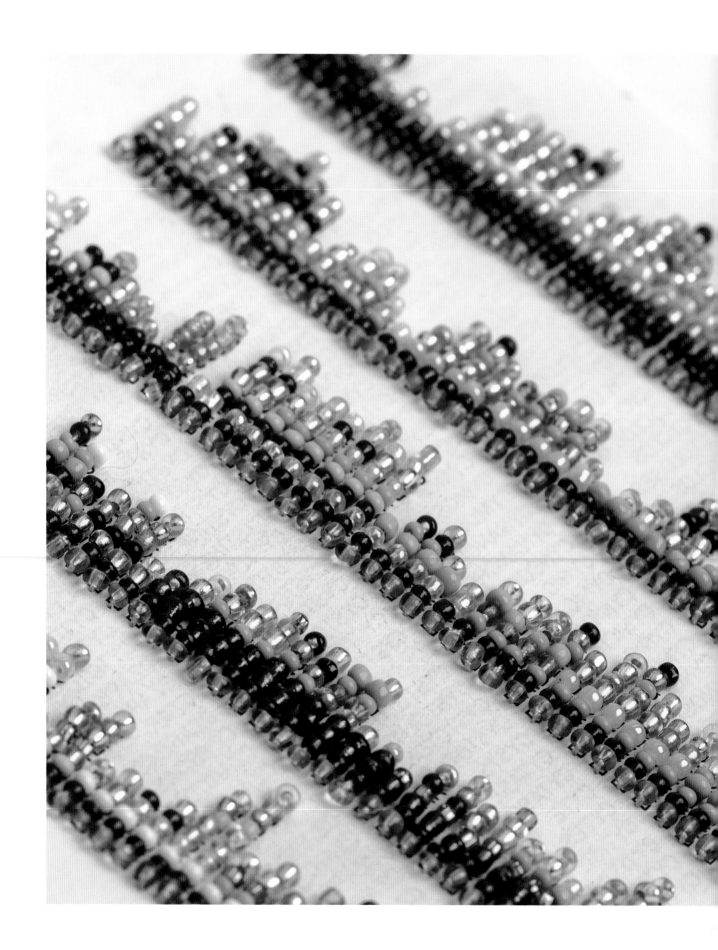

these are clues that we pick up on unconsciously, our minds automatically attempting to decode.

These pieces were far more time-consuming to make than some of my fabric pieces. Each hole needed to be pre-pierced on the page, and the paper was far more fragile, forcing me to work more slowly to avoid rips or creases. I could have just sewn the beads onto a piece of fabric, creating a replica of the book page or document, but it was important to me that I work onto the original. I like to embroider onto found ephemera, perhaps because it challenges me to work with what I already have. If you also find yourself holding on to a lot of ephemera like me, you might want to turn them into keepsake pieces of art in a similar way.

Opposite: *Scrabble Alphabet* (detail).

Right and below: *Coded Alphabet Letter* (2021). Multi-coloured beads on found paper. 135 × 140mm (5¼ × 5½in)

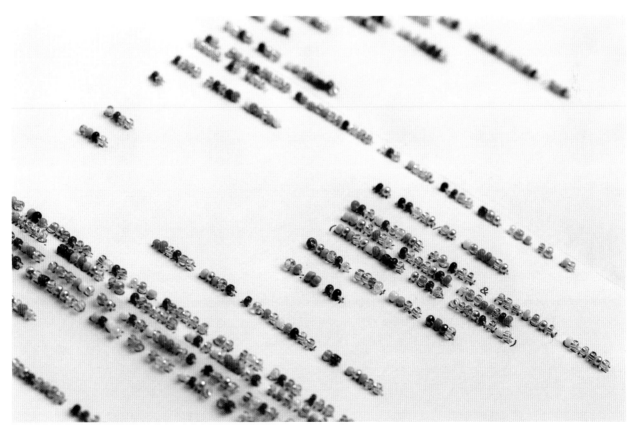

ARTIST'S WORK
—
Sam Meech

Sam Meech is a digital artist from the UK who is now based in Montreal, Canada. I first met him at the National Festival of Making in Blackburn in 2017, where he was selling his binary scarves.

These knitted scarves have famous quotes from the worlds of art and technology translated into binary code using ASCII (short for the American Standard Code for Information Interchange), an encoding system based on 128 symbols including 10 numbers, 26 letters and various punctuation marks.

Binary code is the expression of the alphabet in a series of '0's and '1's. Each letter of the alphabet can be translated into a specific combination of eight '0's and '1's. Sam has demonstrated this through knit by using two colours of yarn to represent either the '0' or the '1'.

This way of translating writing obviously makes the original text much longer, as each letter becomes eight symbols long. For example, the Turing scarf is 24 stitches wide, meaning each row of knitting contains just three letters of the quote.

Although in theory, these designs could be made using a punchcard, this project has been completed in collaboration with an industrial knitting company, so the design work has been done digitally. Before knitting, Sam will visualize the outcome of the pattern using a computer program, then use digital software to send this binary pattern to the knitting machine.

The first scarf in this project, the *www.scarf*, was made as a gift for Sir Tim Berners-Lee, the inventor of the World Wide Web, and presented to him at the Open Data Summit in 2014. This particular scarf was made on a Brother KH950i

'Eight hours daily labour is enough for any human being, and under proper arrangements sufficient to afford an ample supply of food, raiment and shelter, or the necessaries and comforts of life, and for the remainder of his time, every person is entitled to education, recreation and sleep.'

ROBERT OWEN, FROM THE FOUNDATION AXIOMS OF THE SOCIETY FOR PROMOTING NATIONAL REGENERATION (1833)

machine, and subsequent scarves have been made using Shima Seiki machines at Unique Knitwear in Manchester. The *www.scarf* contains a quote from a memo Berners-Lee wrote in 1989, 'The system must allow any sort of information to be entered. Another person must be able to find the information, sometimes without knowing what he is looking for.' Subsequent scarves contain quotes from Alan Turing, Ada Lovelace and Herbert Read.

Sam's *Punchcard Economy* is another interesting project. Based on the heritage of the North West's textile industry, it is a machine-knitted banner based on the slogan 'Eight hours labour, eight hours recreation, eight hours rest', coined by Robert Owen of the Eight-Hour Day movement, which

was a social movement to regulate the working day during the Industrial Revolution in Britain. This piece of work examines contemporary working patterns as compared to the '888' ideal proposed by Owen. The design incorporates data gathered from a range of workers, mainly in the digital, creative and cultural industries.

Participants were invited to log their working week and 200 data sets were gathered. These were then translated into knitted motifs and made into a reinterpretation of the original '8 Hours Labour' banner. Each hour worked outside of the eight-hour structure is expressed as a reverse stitch, which shows up as a glitch in the design. The data showed a significant shift towards a more flexible and in some ways more precarious pattern of working hours, with many people working during evenings or weekends. This piece has particular relevancy as we move towards a fundamental shift in the traditional working day in the wake of the Covid-19 pandemic and the challenges it has brought.

Opposite: Sam Meech, *Binary Knitting*.
Wool. 183 × 23cm (72 × 9in)

Above: Sam Meech, *Punchcard Economy*.
Knitted banner. 3 × 5m (9¾ × 16¼ft)

ARTIST'S WORK
—
Raw Color

Raw Color is a multidisciplinary studio initiated by designers Christoph Brach and Daniera ter Haar and based in Eindhoven, Netherlands, where they work on a number of commissions and self-initiated projects. One such project is *The Cryptographer*. The Cryptographer is a machine that they have created; it has the ability to translate text messages into encoded patterns, and these are then bleached into fabrics to create scarves.

As part of an interactive exhibition called Cryptographer & Encoded Textiles (April 2012), the Cryptographer was on display beside a screen where visitors could send messages. These were then translated by the machine into a code created by the designers and 'drawn' onto fabric using bleach.

To create the code the designers first looked at the frequency of each letter used in the English alphabet and they established that the order of common use, starting with the most commonly used ones, was: etaionshrdlcumwfgypbvkjxqz. With this information, it was possible to estimate compositions and keep a balance between round, square, open and closed shapes.

The bleach process is applied by a pen attached to the print head of the Cryptographer. Reacting differently on each textile dye, the bleach shades vary. The size and scale of the pattern is determined by the number of words sent to the printer and the end result is a scarf that contains a pattern that is determined by a personal message.

Personal messages are increasingly sent digitally: intangible, floating in the air, only readable on a screen. The Cryptographer generates pattern by translating words into a code. Bleached into fabric, the message becomes tangible – invisible words with a physical impact. Controlled by text messaging, each character is transformed into a specified icon, resulting in ever-changing patterns, depending on the user's input.

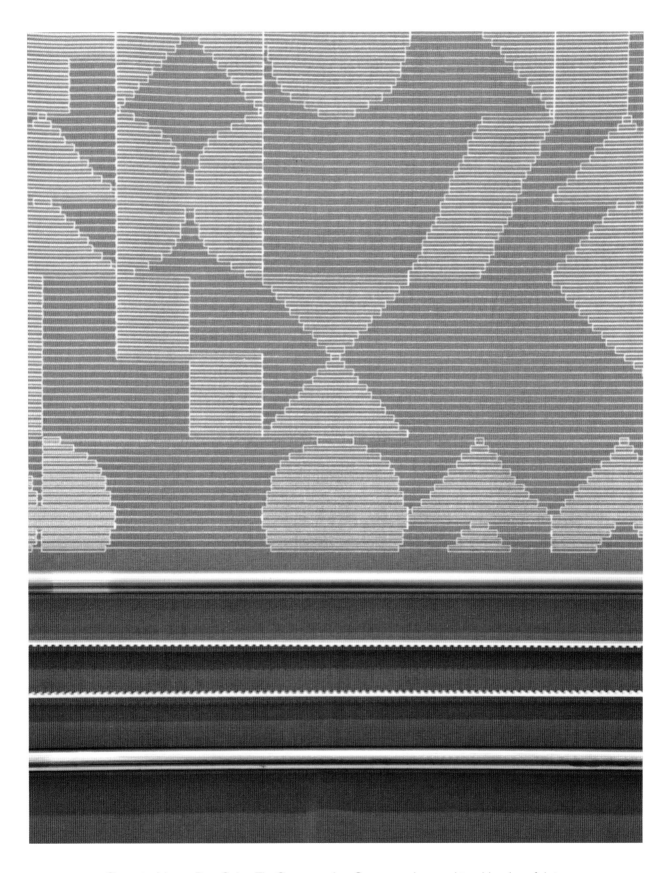

Opposite/above: Raw Color, *The Cryptographer*. Cryptographer machine, bleach on fabric.

ARTIST'S WORK
—
Holly Berry

Based in London, UK, Holly Berry originally trained as a fashion designer, but despairing at the throwaway nature of the industry, her response was to learn how to weave, creating slowly made, meaningful, well-crafted textiles. Holly loves stories and collects treasures, artefacts and fragments of colours, textures, patterns and tales.

In her *Morse Code Weaving* collection of blankets and scarves, Holly uses Morse code to weave hidden and meaningful words such as 'love', 'hold' and 'balance' into the woven cloths, to create modern heirlooms. Using an old Morse code tapping machine as reference, she creates a double woven rectangle to represent a dash and a square to represent a dot, and she leaves small gaps between letters and larger gaps between words. The chosen word is repeated throughout the cloth. Because of the nature of woven fabrics, the secret message is only readable from the front of the cloth, but gives an interesting pattern on the back.

Holly Berry, *LOVE* blanket.
90 per cent merino,
10 per cent cashmere.
150 × 190cm (59 × 74¾in).

DIY Project

Coded Message

You can use binary code to create your own 'hidden message' embroidery. At the back of the book you will find a guide to translating text into binary code, but there are also free services online that allow you to translate passages of text into binary.

Start by choosing the piece of text you wish to translate. It could be a love letter, poem, book passage, to-do list, diary entry, or any piece of writing you feel a strong connection to. As this piece of text will be encoded, it's a good opportunity to use something personal that you might not want to display otherwise.

Remember that each letter of your text will become eight symbols long when translated into binary, so the piece of text will become eight times longer, something to bear in mind when thinking about how long the embroidery might take you, and how much fabric and thread you will need.

Planning the work

Use the graph paper in the back of the book to plan out how your encoded text will look, and mark it up using two symbols or two colours of pen to represent the '0's and '1's. Experiment with the format that your embroidery will take, whether it will be long and thin or square, portrait or landscape. Consider how to space out your symbols: I don't tend to leave any spaces in between, but you may want to split them into sets of eight symbols to represent each letter, or leave spaces between each

word. This is something to experiment with on your graph paper.

Once you have decided on the format for your embroidery, it is almost time to stitch, but first you need to decide how you will differentiate the '0's from the '1's. In my binary beaded diaries, I used two colours of beads, but you might want to use two colours of thread; or perhaps you will keep the same colour of thread but use two different stitches. Base your decision on whatever you feel is the best way to represent your chosen text.

Mindful stitching

Remember, this will be a fairly time-consuming piece of work to complete; it isn't something to be rushed through. Use the time to really connect with your piece of writing. I often find that during mindful stitch sessions I remember things that were previously lost, so let your mind wander and enjoy.

In my example, I have chosen the handwritten message from a greetings card I received. I firstly translated this into binary code, then plotted out the binary code onto graph paper using red and blue pens: I wanted my design to finish in a solid block, so played around with the layout a little bit. I then stitched the design onto fabric, using a simple straight line stitch and blue and red threads, to match my graph paper design. I prefer to use an evenweave fabric for this kind of work as it makes it easier to follow a grid format and to keep track

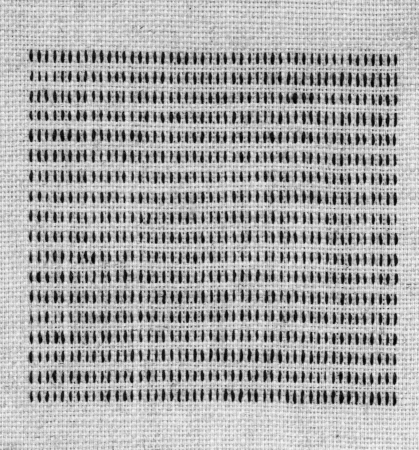

Coded Message project. Red and blue cotton on linen. 135 × 140mm (5¼ × 5½in)

of the stitches, but if you have a special piece of sentimental fabric that links to the text you are translating, this would be a lovely base for your embroidery.

It can sometimes help to mark off the stitches on your graph paper plan as you go, so you can keep track of where you are up to. I chose to sew all the blue stitches first, then all the red, but you could thread two needles, one with each colour, and sew them in tandem; just be careful that they don't get tangled up on the back of your fabric.

Your final piece of work will be an abstract embroidery, and its secret message will only be known to you and those you chose to share it with.

Right: Coded Message project (detail).

Below: The stitches marked out on paper before stitching.

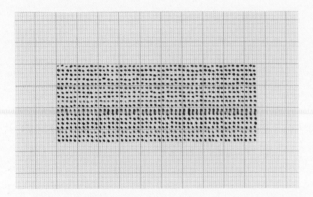

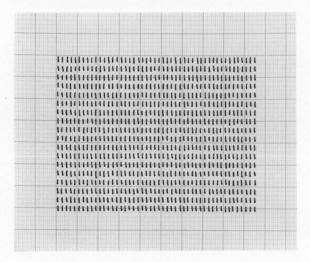

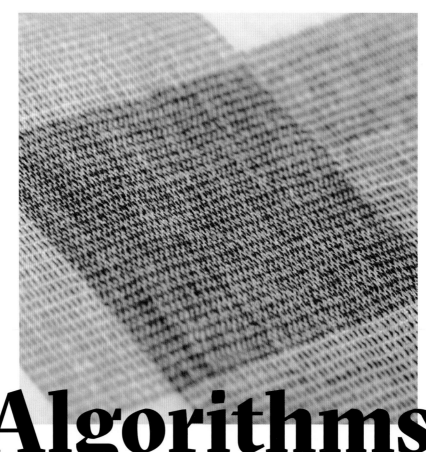

Algorithms

'Art is pattern informed by sensibility.'

HERBERT READ

By definition, the word 'algorithm' refers to a process or set of rules that is followed to produce an outcome, and the outcome is dictated by the constraints set at the beginning. Commonly, this is used to refer to a kind of computer programming, but I am interested in examining it from a textile perspective.

Unlike drawing or painting, where there is an inherent freedom, I have found that textile art lends itself to rule-following. For example, with knit, weave, crochet or lacemaking, if you don't follow the basic foundations of the technique, unchanged for centuries, the whole structure would fall apart. Perhaps this is why this sort of art can sometimes be devalued to 'craft', because it takes longer to cultivate your own style.

For the most part, everyone starts off in the same way, following a pattern created by someone else, and it can be more of a challenge to find your own voice. These are skills for which there are certain building blocks that need to be taught, and it can be harder to work from imagination alone. This results in a deluge of similar pieces of work, and the challenge is to put your own spin on the process; but when you do, it presents new opportunities. Any discipline based on rules comes with the instinctive need to push these boundaries to see how far they can be stretched, and what will emerge as a result.

Personally, I enjoy working in this way because it takes the pressure off my own decision-making. Ironically, there is something freeing about working within constraints, and I find that it makes me more creative. By setting out some parameters to work within, some of the indecisive background noise is eliminated, allowing me to focus more clearly on getting my message across. I first discovered this when I was studying for my MA. I was struggling with some self-doubt and found that I would constantly second-guess my work and my ideas, which was really hindering my creativity. I decided that if I followed some set rules that dictated the direction of the work, then even if I didn't like the outcome, it didn't matter.

This was a turning point for me, when I realized that my work was more about the ideas and the process as opposed to the final result. To have the outcome be dictated by a kind of handmade algorithm was incredibly liberating and freed me up to take more creative risks, and there was also a sense of satisfying my own curiosity. Rather than having a vision in my mind of how a piece would ultimately turn out (which can cause disappointment when it doesn't go to plan), I found a real joy in starting a piece of work, genuinely having no idea how it would end. This approach surprised me: I am not an impromptu person and working like this went against every aspect of my structured personality, but this became my spontaneous outlet, and my confidence flourished as a result.

Mapping the Sky (detail): see page 94.

Ada Lovelace

There is a very interesting textile history to the algorithm. Ada Lovelace is widely considered to have created the first piece of computer programming, and she was inspired to create this algorithm after seeing a Jacquard weaving machine in operation.

Woven fabrics are created by the crossing over of two perpendicular threads, known as the warp and weft. The warp threads are held in tension, while the weft threads are passed over and under to create an interlocking structure. When patterned fabrics are created, the threads need to weave together in a very specific formation to produce the design, a process that was initially very time-consuming, and therefore expensive, until the invention of the Jacquard machine.

The Jacquard machine, patented in 1804, is a device that can be fitted to a loom, which then becomes known as a Jacquard loom. Jacquard looms allow complex designs to be woven with ease through the use of punchcards, which are fed into the device. Punchcards are stiff pieces of paper with holes punched out of them, corresponding to the design of the weave, and the position of these holes determines which warp threads are lifted by the loom to allow the weft threads to pass beneath.

With the introduction of these punchcards, once a pattern had been designed, it could be replicated quickly and accurately on the looms, and this revolutionized the production of woven fabrics.

The punchcards used on the Jacquard looms paved the way for modern computer programming as they inspired modern-day binary code. Jacquard looms use a two-symbol system (punched hole versus no punched hole) in the same way that modern binary uses '0' or '1', and this is why they are considered to be the predecessors of the computers of today.

Ada Lovelace worked alongside Charles Babbage on the first computer, known as the Analytical Engine, and because she wrote the first algorithm to be used with this machine, she is widely considered to be the original computer programmer. While Babbage envisaged his machine to be used purely for calculations, Lovelace described her approach as 'poetical science' and explored options for it beyond just numbers; she felt that it could even be capable of creating music. She is quoted as saying, 'the analytical machine weaves algebraic patterns, just as the Jacquard loom weaves flowers and leaves'.

Rolling Dice project:
see page 108.

Overlapping Number Series

The *Overlapping Number* series comprises some of my first textile pieces based around algorithms. I had an idea that I wanted to make some work using blocks of overlaid stitches, but it isn't in my nature to simply begin stitching randomly sized blocks, so I was looking for some data-driven research to back it up. At the same time, I bought a book from a charity shop that I really wanted to use in a project, *Chambers's Seven-Figure Mathematical Tables*. When I had seen it on the shelf, it had really appealed to me and I had to take it home, where I discovered I had an identical copy, which should tell you something about how strong its pull was!

The book comprises tables of numbers ranging from logarithms to horizon distances, and, although I didn't understand how to use them for their intended purpose, I thought they would be perfect for randomly generating the numbers I needed for my project.

Planning the work

I made a viewfinder to allocate me three numbers per page, then I opened the book at random and positioned the viewfinder. I used my three randomly generated numbers as follows: the first indicated the number of blue stitches; the second indicated the number of red stitches; and the third

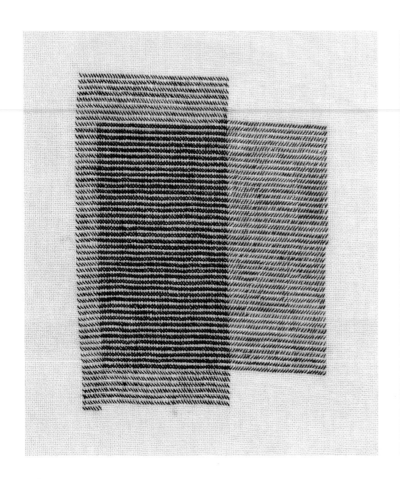

indicated the number of stitches that the two blocks would overlap by. I was completely at the mercy of the viewfinder, and some of the numbers it was producing were very large. For example, one of the blocks was made up of 5,964 stitches. If I had simply been making up the pattern as I went along, then I probably wouldn't have made the block so large. It took me many days to complete, but accepting that this decision was out of my control was a fundamental aspect of the project, and I needed to embrace this system.

I found that following this predetermined pattern, without having to consider the design or composition as I worked, was an extremely mindful activity. The work was repetitive and soothing, and I enjoyed the fact that the art itself was the process, with the outcome secondary to this. Taking the pressure off needing to 'like' the aesthetics of the piece perhaps made me appreciate the result even more.

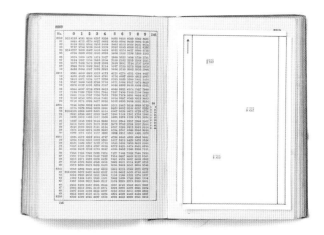

Above: the original book with the overlaid viewfinder.

Below: *Overlapping Number* series (2020). Red and blue cotton on linen. Opposite: 340 × 330mm (13¼ × 13in) Below left: 295 × 265mm (11½ × 10½in) Below right: 375 × 320mm (14¾ × 12½in)

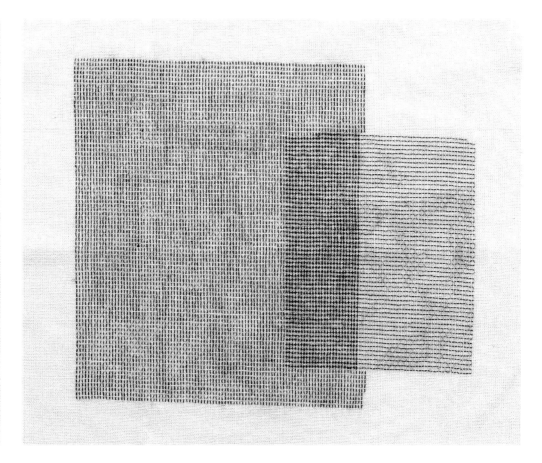

I completed these pieces early on in the first lockdown of 2020. On furlough from work and floundering without my routine, I actually found that having this very time-consuming project to occupy me was calming in a time that was rife with panic and stress.

I repeated this experiment three times and, due to the random nature of my algorithm, the scale of these pieces varied greatly, as did the time they took to stitch. I experimented a little with the stitch style but followed the same rules in terms of colour, thread and format, in order to maintain consistency. Although they sit well together, each piece has subtle differences, alluding to the unique time in which they were created.

Not only were these pieces time-consuming to embroider, but they were also incredibly time-consuming to plan out, something that I hadn't anticipated. I used graph paper to draw each design before I started to stitch, to ensure there were the right number of stitches in each block and that they overlapped by the right amount, while maintaining as close to solid block shapes as possible.

This subject matter is a bit unusual for me as I tend to work with more personal data with more of a storytelling aspect, but it proved to be a good starting point for a far more personal project using my grandad's sweater, which you saw in the Introduction.

Overlapping Number (detail).

Mapping the Sky

A lot of my work has, unconsciously, used the same colour palette. I gravitate towards either monochromes or red, and I tend not to deviate from this. In an attempt to be more deliberate about the work I was producing, I decided to experiment with making the colour choice integral to the piece, using it to enhance the message I was trying to convey rather than choosing colours on autopilot.

I have always been fascinated by the idea of 'capturing' time, to be able to take an intangible everyday experience and make it tangible, something that I can look back on. In this instance, I decided to record a particular day by charting the changing colours of the sky; I thought that this would produce a unique sequence of colours that would set this day apart from any other.

From the same vantage point, I recorded the colour of the same patch of sky through the same window every minute for a whole day. I got up an hour before sunrise, so I could mark the changing shades of dark before daylight, and continued throughout the day until I was satisfied that the darkness was such that the colours would no longer vary.

This was a particularly time-consuming way of collecting data, and if I were to repeat the experiment I would probably use some kind of recording device to capture the colours more efficiently. However, it was important to me that for this first experiment I use my own eyesight and perception, working in an analogue way rather than relying on technology. Ironically, the outcome is probably not a day I would particularly want to recall, given that I spent it sitting in the same spot, but it was more about putting a system in place that I can refer back to in future.

Everyday moments

This piece plays perfectly into my love of championing the everyday. I think that the most important things in our lives are the small, sometimes overlooked, details. These tiny moments build up to give our lives depth and meaning, and without them, the bigger occasions wouldn't exist. These ordinary days pass us by, but retrospectively we realize that they were paving the way for something spectacular.

Not only was this an exercise in archiving, but it was also an example of working in an algorithmic way. If I was in charge of the decision-making, I would perhaps not have chosen to place certain colours side by side, I might have started to overthink the fact that some shades blended together so subtly while others contrasted sharply – but I was following nature's algorithm and that dictated the eventual outcome of the stitching.

I now have a record of this day that I can keep forever. It made me think of the song 'Who Will Buy?' from the musical *Oliver!*, and about the special uniqueness of any given day and the desire to keep it safe, because without something physical to hold on to, we can never experience it again. While I let go of control in terms of the outcome of the piece, I gained control over the potential loss of memories as time passes us by.

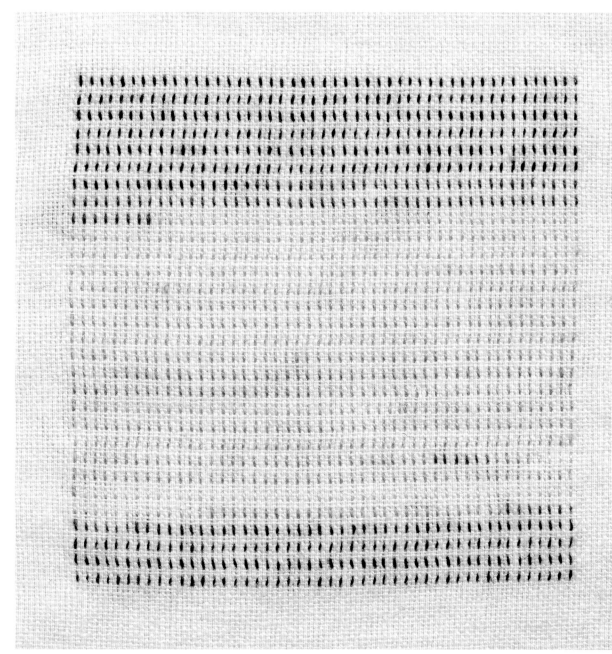

Mapping the Sky (2017). Embroidery thread on linen. 150 × 140mm (6 × 5½in)

Mapping the Sky (detail).

ARTIST'S WORK
—
Richard McVetis

Richard McVetis is a Royal College of Art graduate living and working in London, UK. His meticulous drawings and embroideries are rooted in process and precision. With *Variations of a Stitched Cube* (2017), he has produced a body of work that is a perfect example of the 'handmade algorithm' that I am so intrigued by. He has created a set of rules up front and followed them throughout the project, leading him to an outcome that is formulaic yet beautifully organic, the final realization of the collection reflecting the systematic driving force behind the initial idea, as he describes here:

'*Variations of a Stitched Cube is a series of hand-embroidered cubes based on the composite number 60 and the systems in which we measure time. Each cube measures 60mm in height, width and depth – the scale and proportion relating to "the hand" and the process of making itself. The cubes are presented in a sequence, recording time through multiples of hand-embroidered dots measured in increasing and enforced increments of one hour, starting with the first cube at one hour of stitching and finishing on the sixtieth and final cube with 60 hours of stitching.*

The cubes show time, an ever-present invisible force, through form as both logical and playful. Defined by their materials and created through the random process of embroidery and the action of

the hand, generating variations with self-imposed restrictions to imply and manifest the passage of time. The presentation and installation of the work in a grid format give the impression of uniformity but also of infinity. This grid layout and the system of production offers me a rational way to organize the chaos of nature. It requires us to focus on perception, on process, but also declares a freedom from having to follow any rules.

Variations of a Stitched Cube draws inspiration from two sources: firstly, the origin and system of recording time and the number 60; secondly, the work and theories of minimalist artist Sol LeWitt, particularly his essay "Paragraphs on Conceptual Art" and the following two sentences:

"When an artist uses a conceptual form of art, it means that all of the planning and decisions are made beforehand, and the execution is a perfunctory affair."

"The idea becomes a machine that makes the art."

Taking the number 60, the unit in which we measure seconds and minutes, or a composite, I devised an artwork with a series of algorithms:
– Use black cotton thread and wool fabric to embroider a cube measuring 60 × 60 × 60mm.
– Start at the same point.
– Use only one stitch technique.
– Stitch for increasing increments of one hour, i.e., the first cube at one hour of stitching and finish on the sixtieth and final cube with 60 hours of stitching.'

Richard McVetis, *Variations of a Stitched Cube*. Cubes: hand embroidery, cotton on wool. 6 × 6 × 6cm (2⅜in × 2⅜in × 2⅜in). Sculpture: MDF and birch ply. 120 × 150 × 85cm (47¼ × 59 × 33½in)

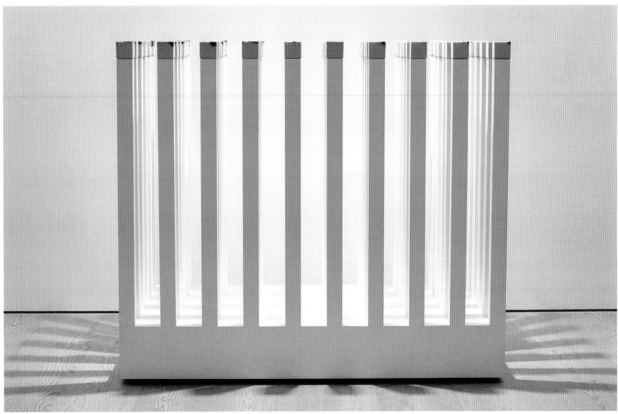

ARTIST'S WORK
—
Evelin Kasikov

Evelin Kasikov is a book designer from Estonia who has been based in London, UK since 2006. As part of a personal project, Evelin has looked at combining book design with stitch, taking the rapid process of digital print and combining it with the painstaking technique of hand embroidery. Two examples of this crossover of techniques are *CMYK Embroidery* (2007 onwards) and *XXXX Swatchbook* (2016).

CMYK is a colour model used in digital printing, also known as four-colour printing, using inks C (cyan), M (magenta), Y (yellow) and K (key, or black). In the four-colour printing process, these four shades are combined as patterns of small overlapping dots (or pixels) to create the full spectrum of colour that we see in digital printing. In Evelin's version, however, the 'pixels' are made up of hand-embroidered cross stitches, using threads in the CMYK colours. Evelin has used this approach across a number of embroidered samples in her own portfolio, as well as for commercial and private commissions for a range of clients. From a distance, these pieces create the optical illusion of being printed because our brains recognize the construct of the CMYK colour palette, and the result is that the work reads like a swatchbook, and only on closer inspection can you see that it is actually embroidery.

The *XXXX Swatchbook* is a book about print, and yet it contains no trace of ink. This book, which has taken the past six years to make, demonstrates the range of colours that can be achieved with the four-colour printing process, but rather than being digitally reproduced, every aspect of the book is hand embroidered. The pages suddenly have a tactile and three-dimensional quality; they take

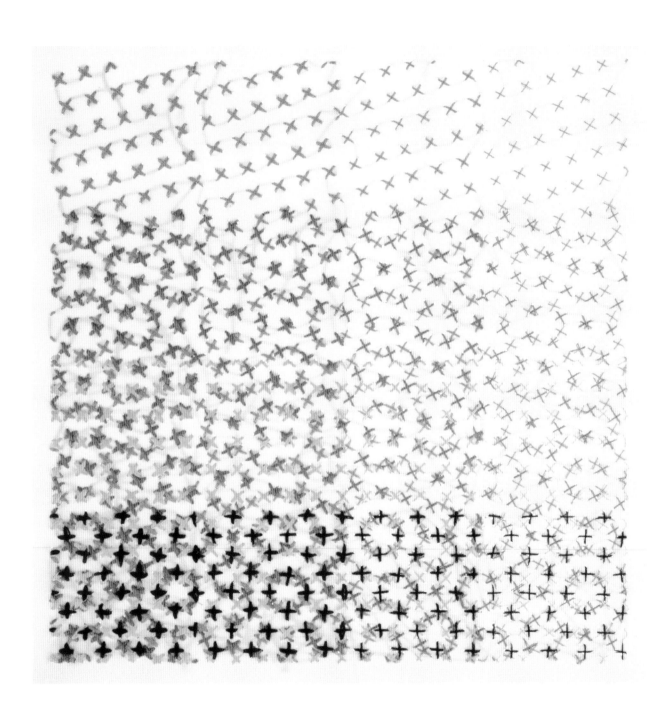

Evelin Kasikov, *CMYK Embroidery*. CMYK embroidery thread on paper.

the convenience of printing and suddenly make it laborious and handmade. In this piece, Evelin has created her own reference guide, as a digital creator might use a Pantone swatchbook. She has something to refer back to, to inform the outcome of every combination of stitch and colour; the *XXXX Swatchbook* contains 400 combinations by overlaying and rotating handmade halftone screens.

Evelin Kasikov, *XXXX Swatchbook*.
CMYK embroidery thread on paper.

When describing her practice, Evelin says:

'*I'm interested in embroidery as a precise, mathematical process. Coming from a graphic design background I wanted to explore the world of graphic design – typography, colour, grid – in handmade form. CMYK embroidery is essentially a handmade printing technique that replicates four-colour offset printing. This kind of logical, analytical approach to embroidery fascinates me, this is where I find beauty.*'

ARTIST'S WORK
—
Channing Hansen

Channing Hansen, an artist based in Los Angeles, California, USA, combines an interest in craft, science and technology to create his work. Contemporary technology and age-old techniques coexist within Channing's work as he blends mathematical algorithms with traditional hand-knitting techniques. The yarn used in its production is hand-spun fibre, mostly wool derived from breeds of sheep that are currently classified as conservation breeds, meaning that they suffer varying degrees of endangerment due to monoculture and factory farming. Channing hopes that by using fibre that has been humanely and sustainably sheared from these sheep, he can invite others to reconsider the importance of biological diversity, even among domesticated species. Channing keeps track of every kind of fibre that is spun into the yarn, including the names of the sheep whose fleece he has used.

Channing's *Homeostatic Havoc* pieces are based on a computer-generated algorithm that he has written himself. It is used to create a 'score', which in turn determines the pattern of the knitted textiles, by instructing the kind of fibre blend, colour, stitch, pattern, or mistake to make at any given moment while he knits. The outcomes are knitted 'paintings' that are tangible reactions to the mathematical algorithm he has put in place. The colours and textures of the knitted surfaces range from loose to tight, raw to refined, thick to thin, chunky to fine, and are all determined by this initial set of rules. This is not to say that there is no artist-input for these pieces, and it is not a one-way process. Channing becomes engaged in a feedback loop that sees him making subtle, perhaps unconscious, adjustments in response to a wide range of personal and external variables, as well as information derived from observing the work itself being made.

Channing is interested in the idea that humans themselves embody an infinite number of potential algorithms. We are increasingly familiar with the ways in which everything, from our personal relationships to our political preferences, can be expressed as and shaped by algorithms. This raises questions about precisely what it means to be human at a time when we seem to be either merging with or replaced by artificial intelligence. Talking about *Homeostatic Havoc* in 2020, Channing elaborates:

'*While sheltering at home during the pandemic, I was obsessing about how even slight changes in variables can cause explosive changes in a system while it seeks its equilibrium – whether it's populations of certain animals skyrocketing after their main predators have been over-hunted or the spread of Covid-19 (especially when safety protocols are not observed). This phenomenon is also reflected in how thoughts propagate through one's neurons; for instance, the proliferation of certain types of thoughts can lead to disorders such as anxiety, OCD, etc.*

The algorithm was based upon the bifurcation theory of dynamical chaos. It's a mathematical diagram of how natural systems reach equilibrium. It connects neuron firing, fractals and animal populations.

Basically, the algorithm helped me to connect what was going on in my internal world with what was happening externally, to understand how sudden disequilibrium externally produces the same thing internally. Both realms seek to re-establish equilibrium – a pursuit that, of late, has seemed to be thwarted at every turn. (I write this as California is consumed by an unheard-of number of wildfires; the air all around is smoky and the light has an ominous orange cast.)

The selection of yarns was entirely determined by what was in my studio when the pandemic hit. If there is any harmony or disharmony in their relationship, it is entirely circumstantial (rather than deliberate).'

Channing Hansen, *Homeostatic Havoc*. Hand-spun, hand-dyed wool;
synthetic fibres and redwood. 163 × 163cm (64 × 64in)

ARTIST'S WORK
—
Michelle Stephens

Michelle Stephens is a textile artist and lecturer from Moira, Northern Ireland, UK who has a wide range of qualifications including a BA First-Class Honours degree, a Master's degree and a practice-based PhD. Currently, Michelle is also a member of the internationally recognized 62 Group of textile artists.

For her project *Coded Cloth*, Michelle collaborated with The Silk Museum and Paradise Mill, Macclesfield, Cheshire, to utilize archival pattern books from their collection. They provide source material for her to creatively explore and interpret pattern designs for digital-led Jacquard weaving through generative design

and programming methods. Michelle takes these original archive patterns and reanimates them using computer algorithms. The algorithms introduce a glitch that alters the original design while keeping it identifiable, then the newly configured design is recreated in weave to bring the process full circle. This project fuses the traditional techniques of Jacquard weaving with the contemporary skill of computer programming.

Manipulation with algorithms

Michelle's process involves using a computer algorithm to manipulate the original archival design. The algorithm uses two code blocks (a code block is a set of instructions used within computer programming). The first code block is called the 'digital data bend'. This takes the original archive material and plays with order and chaos within the image by intentionally introducing a glitch. The code block acts as a compressor, ripping apart the original image and piecing it back together again, pixelating certain parts and leaving others clear. The actual pattern is still visible, but the composition is fragmented and reconfigured, almost like a collage or strip-piecing patchwork. During this process the core internal oppositions exist within the work: geometric and organic, construction and deconstruction, order and chaos. There is an element of chance in the creation of this work as the code inevitably dictates what is kept and what isn't. The code produces several outcomes, by distorting the design by varied percentages; for example, 10 per cent distortion would be very close to the original design, but 90 per cent might render it entirely unrecognizable. Michelle then chooses the most successful outcome, which is then taken to the second code block.

The second code block forms repeat and non-repeat patterns with a second set of rules. The

Reanimated textile design using Processing as a design tool.

Michelle Stephens, *Coded Cloth*. Silk weaving with black warp. 2.5 × 1.5m (8¼ × 5ft)

straight repeat option in this code is closely linked to how a Jacquard repeat works across the width of the cloth on traditional looms. From this digital design outcome, the final designs are chosen according to the 'parameters of success' developed by Michelle. Although the design possibilities from the algorithm are infinite, there are practical limitations when it comes to reproducing them on the loom. At this point, Michelle's existing tacit and material knowledge is required before the outcome can be realized, and the context of the final work is negotiated constantly throughout the entire design process. Furthermore, due to Michelle's existing weaving knowledge, some designs can be tweaked in the translation to cloth stage, where other simpler structures can be used to meet end use restrictions. Non-repeat designs are harder to translate and will ultimately cost more to produce.

The reanimation of archival material provides a method of interpretation of the traditional source material into contemporary relevance, offering something more in-depth than merely digitizing an archive – it allows interaction, and this creates future sustainability by attracting new audiences.

Rolling Dice

To create an algorithmic embroidery, we need to create a kind of handmade algorithm – a system to dictate the outcome of the embroidery and what it will look like. This algorithm will provide you with your own collection of stitches, in a pattern and formation dictated by the initial set of rules.

Some of the easiest ways to randomly generate information are by drawing names out of a hat, tossing a coin, or rolling a dice. In this instance, I decided to roll a dice. First, choose six different stitches, and number them one to six. You can use the same stitches as I have done here, or chose your favourites. In my example, I have chosen six stitches that are all the same size – each one takes up a three-by-three grid space on the fabric, which means that whatever configuration of stitches I end up with, each row will remain the same length and all the stitches will line up. I like to work like this as it ensures that my embroidery will always fall into a neat block. If this is something you want to achieve, you will find it easiest to work on an evenweave fabric.

I began to stitch by rolling a dice once to determine the type of stitch, and then again to determine the number of those stitches; so, for example, if I roll a 1, that dictates a cross stitch, and then if that is followed by rolling a 5, it means I need to do five cross stitches. I didn't plan this out on paper beforehand, I just kept the dice by the side of my embroidery and rolled before making each set of stitches. But you may want to use graph paper to plan out the stitches you are going to select, especially if you are wanting them to all take up the same amount of space. Or you may want to plan out the whole piece of embroidery in advance using a dice and pen and paper, and then stitch afterwards.

Planning your format

In terms of the format of the stitching, that is up to you. You might want each 'throw' to be stitched on a separate line, or you might prefer the layout of a square block of stitching, as in my example. If you want to make the stitching into a solid block, you will need to keep going until you roll a number that allows you to finish at the end of the row; for example, if you have three spaces left at the end of the row and you roll a 3, you will finish neatly, but if you roll a 4 you will end up on the next line, so you'll need to throw again. Or you might choose to put another constraint in place, and say, for example, that you will roll the dice 50 times and stop after that, regardless of the format. You might not have an end point in mind, preferring to keep it ongoing. This project works really well as a mindful stitch activity because you don't need to think or plan as the algorithm will do that for you. When you need a short creative reprieve, or an activity to get you into the habit of stitching when facing a creative block, this is a useful piece to pick up.

Rolling Dice project. Red embroidery thread on linen. 130 × 130mm (5 × 5in)

Rolling Dice project (detail).

DIY Project

Journey Algorithm

For this project I will show you how to use an algorithm to create an embroidery based on a journey. We are going to represent this journey through a unique colour palette collected en route. The journey you chose is up to you: it could be a favourite walk, a daily commute or a special trip taken using any form of transport. First you need to devise a set of rules for how you will collect your colours (this will become your algorithm), then you will follow these rules to gather the colours for your embroidery.

For my embroidery, I used a walk that I took regularly during the first lockdown in 2020. This particular route boasts a vast array of colourful spring flowers, so I decided to incorporate these into my algorithm. I set the rule that I would follow my route as normal, stopping every 10 minutes to record the colour of the nearest flower, and over the course of my walk I collected 15 flowers. These colours, in the order that I collected them, became the palette for my embroidery. The only equipment I used to gather my data was my phone. I set a timer to go off every 10 minutes to make it easy to keep track of my time, then each time I stopped I used my phone to take a photograph of the chosen flower.

The finished sampler is a colourful homage to a walk that carries a lot of meaning for me, and it is also a one-off representation of a period of time that cannot be repeated. It is interesting to work with something so ever-changing as nature. The 'day' that I have captured will never come around again. No matter how many times I repeat

this experiment, I will never end up with the same palette. Factors such as the pace at which I walk, how long it takes the lights to change when I want to cross the road, whether I stop to talk to someone, will all impact on where I am positioned when the 10-minute timer goes off, and thus what colour I end up photographing. And then there are the flowers themselves, also transient. If I completed the walk a few months later, the flowers, and therefore the colours I found, would be different. It would be interesting to complete this exercise once per season to see what different colour combinations I end up with.

Creating your own project

You might want to follow my example and photograph flowers along a favourite walking route, but equally you might want to stop and collect every colourful front door you see as you walk through a town, or on a car journey you might be looking at road signs or passing vehicles – it doesn't matter what rules you set, as long as you stick to them. Collect the data in whatever way feels easiest for you. You might want to take a photograph each time, or you might be happy to just make notes of the colours in a notebook, maybe using a set of coloured pencils.

The types of thread you choose will depend on your subject matter. For colours from nature, for example, you might want bright colours or variegated threads, but if you are looking at roadworks, etc., you could do something really

Journey Algorithm project (detail).

Journey Algorithm project. Multi-
coloured embroidery thread on linen.
110 × 110mm (4½ × 4½in)

Opposite: Photographs taken along the
route, and threads used in the project.

interesting with neon and metallic threads. If you are someone who likes to dye their own threads, you could use the flowers you collect to dye the threads, then use these threads for your stitching, to record your findings.

Once you have used your algorithm to determine your colour palette and chosen your threads, you are ready to stitch. I have 15 colours to include, so one stitch per colour would make a very small sampler, and I have chosen to create two rows of stitch per chosen colour. I have used mostly blocks of colour, but some of the flowers I have photographed are two distinctly different colours, so I have captured that by alternating my thread colours. This might be something you want to consider, too, or maybe you will choose to record the most dominant colour, or the one you feel most drawn to. This is your algorithm so you make the rules to best suit you!

What type of stitch will you use? I have chosen a cross stitch as it gives me the freedom to combine two colours within one stitch if I wish to, but you may have another favourite.

How you ultimately decide to display the data you collect is down to you. Enjoy finding a colour palette to represent you.

Conclusion

The aim of this book is to encourage you to find a new and playful means of storytelling using your personal data. Recording information slowly and meditatively through stitch is a great way to honour the quieter moments in our lives, and to acknowledge the important part they play in our overall narrative. Use the DIY projects as a starting point to develop your own practice, and explore the endless opportunities for commemorating and archiving your experiences in a tactile way. I hope that you discover some exciting artists within these pages who will inspire you to look at your world through a new lens, noticing patterns and bringing to life forgotten memories.

The message I want you to take away is: don't wait for a significant milestone before you start to document, because everyday life is worthy of celebration.

Graph Paper

Here is a selection of graph paper at different scales for you to copy and use in your work.

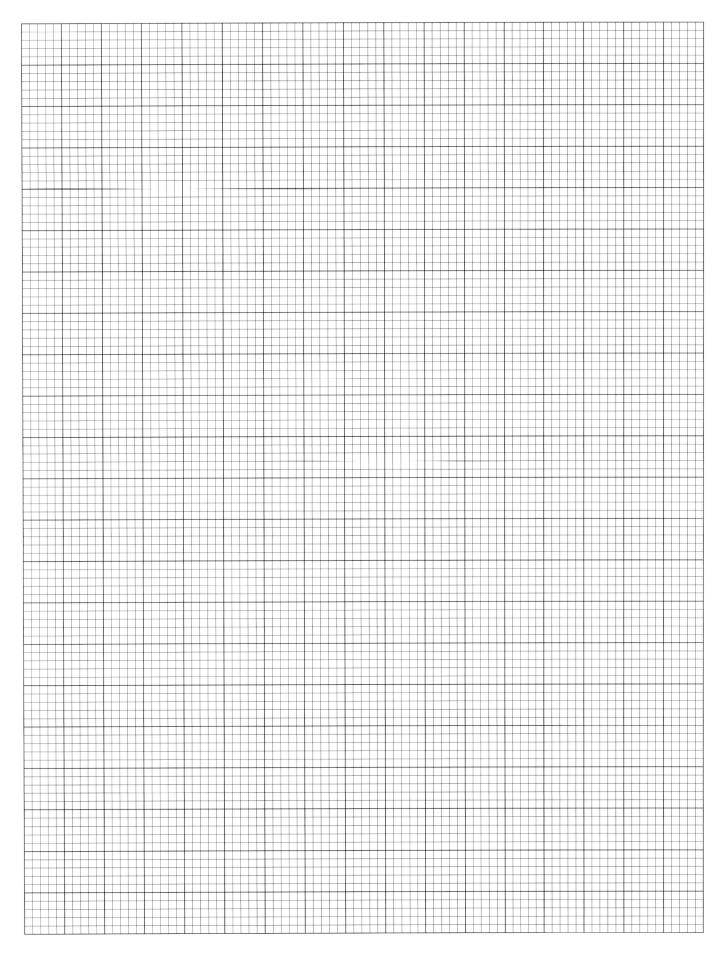

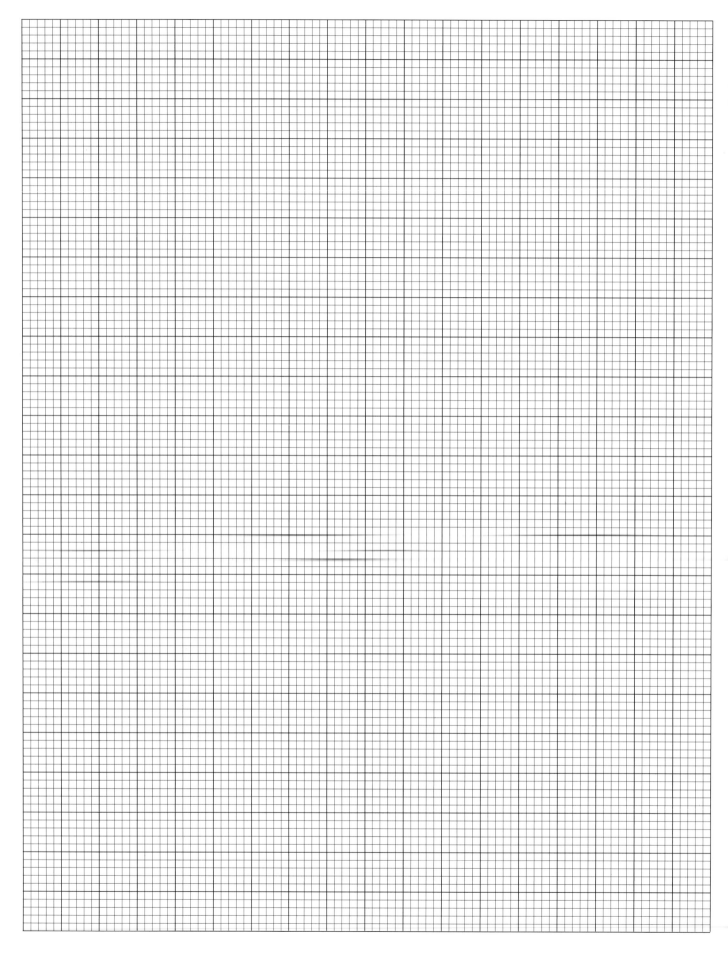

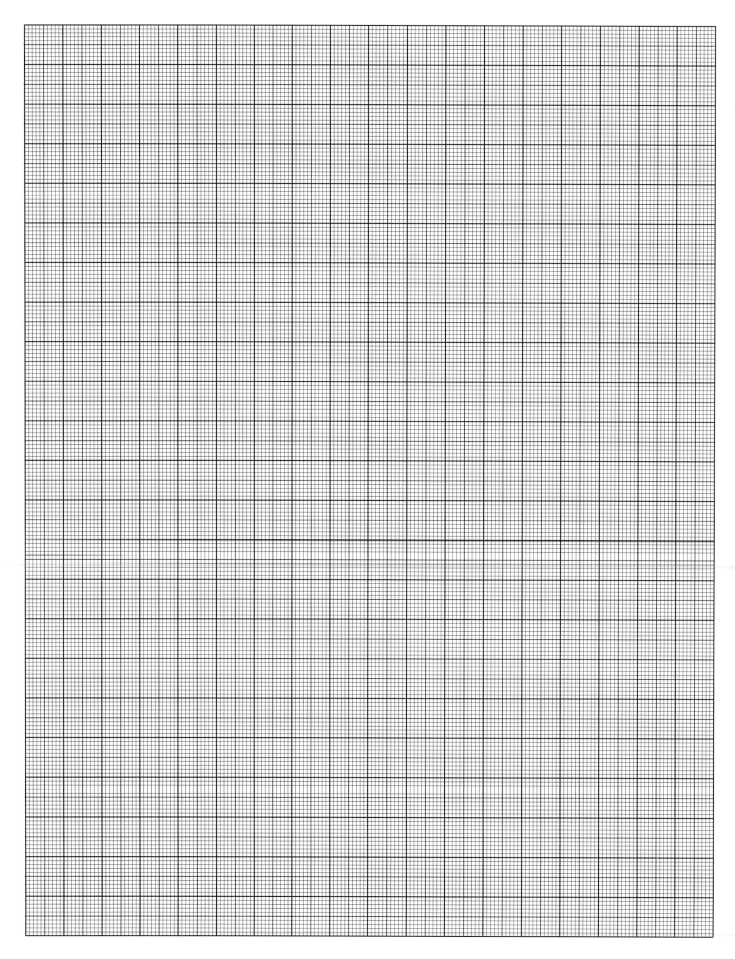

Binary Code Translator

A	01000001	a	01100001	0	00110000
B	01000010	b	01100010	1	00110001
C	01000011	c	01100011	2	00110010
D	01000100	d	01100100	3	00110011
E	01000101	e	01100101	4	00110100
F	01000110	f	01100110	5	00110101
G	01000111	g	01100111	6	00110110
H	01001000	h	01101000	7	00110111
I	01001001	i	01101001	8	00111000
J	01001010	j	01101010	9	00111001
K	01001011	k	01101011		
L	01001100	l	01101100		
M	01001101	m	01101101		
N	01001110	n	01101110		
O	01001111	o	01101111		
P	01010000	p	01110000		
Q	01010001	q	01110001		
R	01010010	r	01110010		
S	01010011	s	01110011		
T	01010100	t	01110100		
U	01010101	u	01110101		
V	01010110	v	01110110		
W	01010111	w	01110111		
X	01011000	x	01111000		
Y	01011001	y	01111001		
Z	01011010	z	01111010		

Morse Code Translator

A	● ▬	0	▬ ▬ ▬ ▬ ▬
B	▬ ● ● ●	1	● ▬ ▬ ▬ ▬
C	▬ ● ▬ ●	2	● ● ▬ ▬ ▬
D	▬ ● ●	3	● ● ● ▬ ▬
E	●	4	● ● ● ● ▬
F	● ● ▬ ●	5	● ● ● ● ●
G	▬ ▬ ●	6	▬ ● ● ● ●
H	● ● ● ●	7	▬ ▬ ● ● ●
I	● ●	8	▬ ▬ ▬ ● ●
J	● ▬ ▬ ▬	9	▬ ▬ ▬ ▬ ●
K	▬ ● ▬		
L	● ▬ ● ●		
M	▬ ▬		
N	▬ ●		
O	▬ ▬ ▬		
P	● ▬ ▬ ●		
Q	▬ ▬ ● ▬		
R	● ▬ ●		
S	● ● ●		
T	▬		
U	● ● ▬		
V	● ● ● ▬		
W	● ▬ ▬		
X	▬ ● ● ▬		
Y	▬ ● ▬ ▬		
Z	▬ ▬ ● ●		

Contributing artists

Jordan Cunliffe

www.jordancunliffe.co.uk
jordanamycunliffe@gmail.com
Instagram: @artisan_embroidery

Ahree Lee

www.ahreelee.com

Channing Hansen

www.stephenfriedman.com/
artists/40-channing-hansen/

Evelin Kasikov

www.evelinkasikov.com
studio@evelinkasikov.com
Instagram: @evelin_kasikov

Holly Berry

Instagram: @hollyberry_
woventextiles

Laurie Frick

www.lauriefrick.com
Instagram: @lauriefrick

Michelle Stephens

www.michellestephens.co.uk
mail@michellestephens.co.uk
Instagram: @dr_michelle_
stephens
Twitter: @MStephensArtist
Facebook: Michelle Stephens
This body of research has been
further supported by the North
West Consortium Doctorial
Training Partnership.

North
West
Consortium
Doctoral
Training
Partnership

Olivia Johnson

o-j.co
olivia@o-j.co
Instagram: @o_j.co
Twitter: @o_jco

Raw Color

www.rawcolor.nl
info@rawcolor.nl
Instagram: @raw_color_
This project was technically very
complex, due to this we could
never have done it without the
help of dedicated experts. We
are very thankful for the inspiring
and productive collaborations.
The final software and interface
were developed in collaboration
with Remon van den Eijnden
and Peter Bust. The elementary
programming and direct control
elements of the engines was
done by Bart van der Linden.
Studio Watt took care of the
engineering and electronica.
The project was presented for
the first time at Dutch Invertuals
'Retouched' during Salone de
Mobile in Milano from 17–22
April 2012. Initiator and Curator
Wendy Plomp, other participants
Daphna Laurens, Edhv, Mieke
Meijer, Jetske Visser, Jeroen
Wand, Maurizio Montalti,
Kirstie van Noort, Susana
Camara, Mike Thompson,
Adrien Petrucci and Paul Heijnen.

Richard McVetis

www.richardmcvetis.co.uk
Instagram: @richardmcvetis
Variations of a Stitched Cube
supported with funding from the
Arts Council England.

Sam Meech

portfolio.smeech.co.uk
Instagram: @videosmithery
Originally commissioned by
FACT Liverpool and Open Data
Institute, *Punchcard Economy*
has since toured internationally
– significantly to a range of
audiences, from textiles and craft
events (Festival of Making) to art
and critical theory conferences
(Transmediale), Design Biennales
(St Etienne Design Biennale),
and data / technology exhibitions
(Future Everything, Open Data
Institute).

Tempestry Project

www.tempestryproject.com
tempestryproject@gmail.com
Instagram: @tempestryproject
Twitter: @tempestryproj

Index

Picture credits

All photography by Michael Wicks except the following:

27 IanDagnall Computing/Alamy; 40 (left and right), 41, 42 (top and bottom),
43: Laurie Frick; 48 (left and right), 49 (top and bottom): Nimi Einstein; 50, 51: Cecily Brown;
65: The Lady magazine; 74, 75: Sam Meech; 76, 77: Raw Color; 78: Holly Berry;
99 (top and bottom): Yeshen Venema; 100 (left and right), 101: Jan Mahr, Juliet Sheath,
Evelin Kasikov; 105: Mark Blower; 106, 107: Dr Michelle Stephens

Acknowledgements

I would like to thank the following people:

Claire Wellesley-Smith, the catalyst for this book,
 for her generous help and indispensable advice.
Nicola Newman, Tina Persaud and all at Batsford
 for this opportunity.
All of my contributing artists for their inspiring work
 and willingness to share.
Michael Wicks for the beautiful photography.

Mitch for his endless patience and expertise.
My parents, for being my biggest cheerleaders,
 with special thanks to my Mum who trialled all
 the DIY projects in this book.
Finally, Adam; for his unwavering support and
 loveliness.

This book is for Ettilie; the best thing
I have ever made.